池本幹雄

I am a huge cat lover, so I respect Mitsuaki Iwago highly. He is an animal photographer who specializes in cats, famous for the NHK program *Sekai Neko-aruki* (World Cats Travelogue).

He's a celebrity among cat lovers.

The *Cats Travelogue* film version was awesome as well.

Such countless heart-moving scenes that only Iwago-san could capture. He really is a god. My desktop calendar is also Iwago-san's cat series. I use it mainly to keep track of deadlines... Whoops, I'm cutting it close this month too... Later!

–Mikio Ikemoto, 2021

VOLUME 14

SHONEN JUMP EDITION

Creator/Supervisor MASASHI KISHIMOTO
Art by MIKIO IKEMOTO

Translation: Mari Morimoto
Touch-Up Art & Lettering: Snir Aharon
Design: Alice Lewis
Editor: Alexis Kirsch

Printed in the U.S.A.

Published by VIZ Media, LLC
P.O. Box 77010
San Francisco, CA 94107

10 9 8 7 6 5 4 3 2 1
First printing, May 2022

BORUTO -NARUTO NEXT GENERATIONS-

VOLUME 14

Creator/Supervisor
Masashi Kishimoto
Art by
Mikio Ikemoto

Legacy

BORUTO -NARUTO NEXT GENERATIONS- CHARACTERS

Mitsuki

Uchiha Sarada

Uzumaki Boruto

Yamanaka Inojin

Nara Shikadai

Akimichi Cho-Cho

STORY

The Great Ninja War that shook the world and shed much blood is now history. Naruto has become the Seventh Hokage, and the people of Konohagakure Village are enjoying peace. Yet Naruto's son Uzumaki Boruto has a glum life, perhaps due to his father's too-great influence.

But Ohtsutsuki Clan members attack, and leave a mysterious mark, the Karma, on Seventh Hokage Naruto's son Boruto...

Afterwards, Boruto happens upon a young man named Kawaki who bears the same Karma as himself. And it is he who is proven to be what Kara has been calling the Vessel.

In order to place Kawaki under his protection, Naruto moves him into his own home. Boruto and Kawaki keep butting heads, but Kawaki starts acclimating to the Village...

However, Kara shows up to reclaim Kawaki and takes Naruto prisoner. Naruto is successfully rescued, but Boruto's Karma-caused transmutation progresses...

Later, Kara member Amado defects to Konoha! Kashin Koji faces off against Kara ringleader Jigen. During their battle, Jigen takes on his true form of Ohtsutsuki Isshiki. Even with his life running out, Isshiki still possesses overwhelming power, and Naruto and Sasuke struggle against him. Kurama then proposes an ultimate desperation move to Naruto. In order to protect those he loves, Naruto activates this new fighting mode that puts his life at risk...

BORUTO
-NARUTO NEXT GENERATIONS-

VOLUME 14
LEGACY

CONTENTS

Number 52:
Baryon Mode

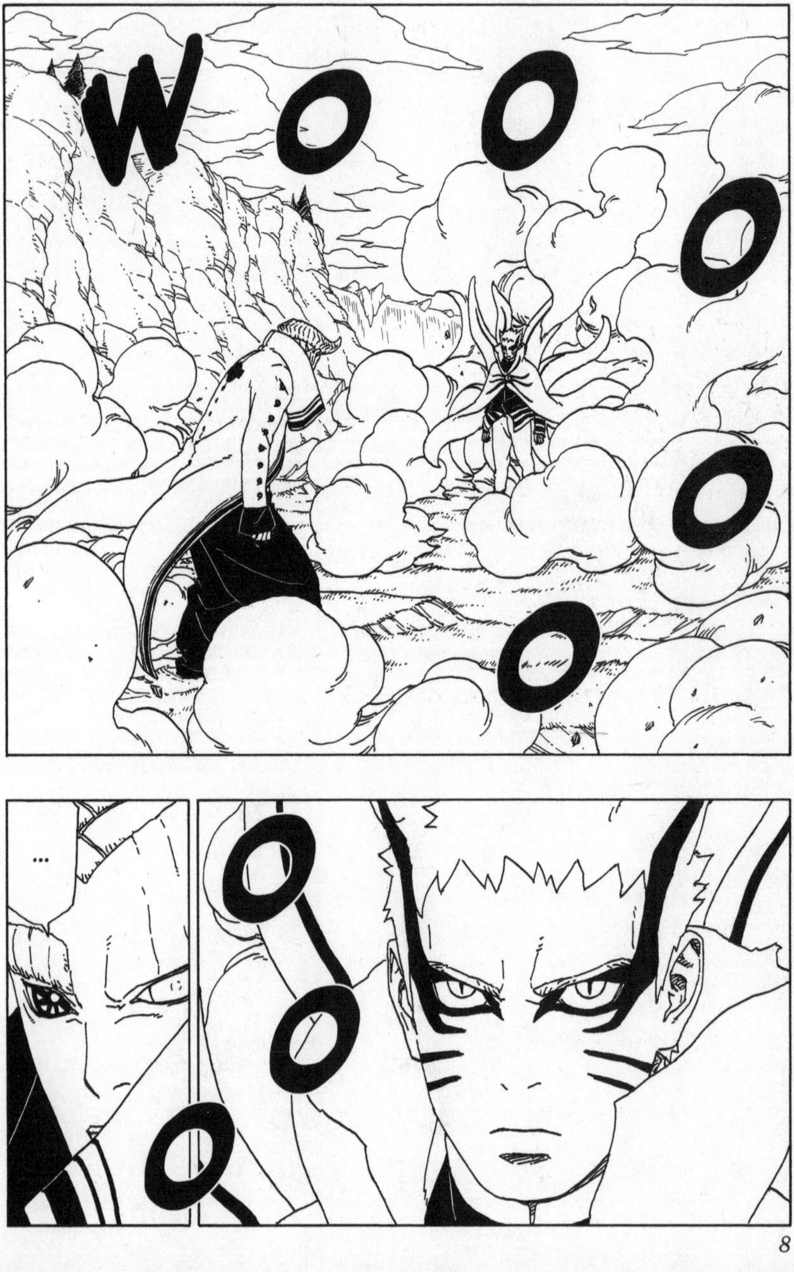

WOOOOO

OOOO

SUCH TREMENDOUS CHAKRA...

WHAT IS IT?!

HE NEVER TOLD ME HE HAD A MOVE LIKE THIS.

HOW COULD HE STILL HAVE SUCH AN ACE UP HIS SLEEVE?

WHY DIDN'T HE USE IT BEFORE?

WO

OOO

THINK OF IT LIKE NUCLEAR FUSION.
IT'S A SIMILAR PRINCIPLE TO HOW THE SUN PRODUCES ENERGY.
...
NUCLEAR FUSION?
WHAT'S THAT?

NEVER MIND. THE THEORY DOESN'T MATTER.
MY CHAKRA AND YOUR CHAKRA ARE SERVING AS THE KERNELS...
...TO PRODUCE A WHOLE OTHER, NEW TYPE OF ENERGY.
THAT'S ALL.

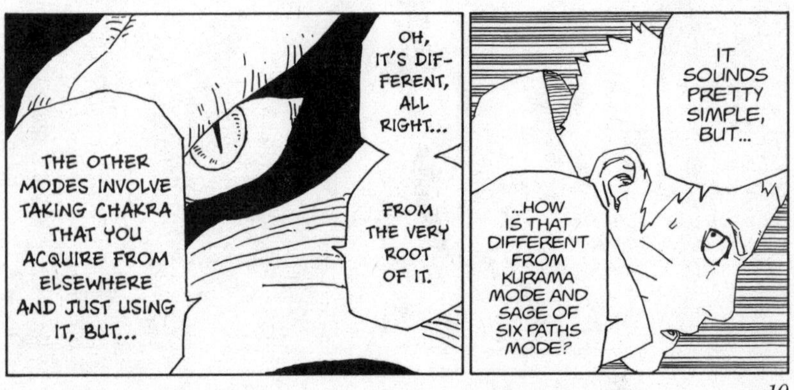
IT SOUNDS PRETTY SIMPLE, BUT...
...HOW IS THAT DIFFERENT FROM KURAMA MODE AND SAGE OF SIX PATHS MODE?
OH, IT'S DIF-FERENT, ALL RIGHT...
FROM THE VERY ROOT OF IT.
THE OTHER MODES INVOLVE TAKING CHAKRA THAT YOU ACQUIRE FROM ELSEWHERE AND JUST USING IT, BUT...

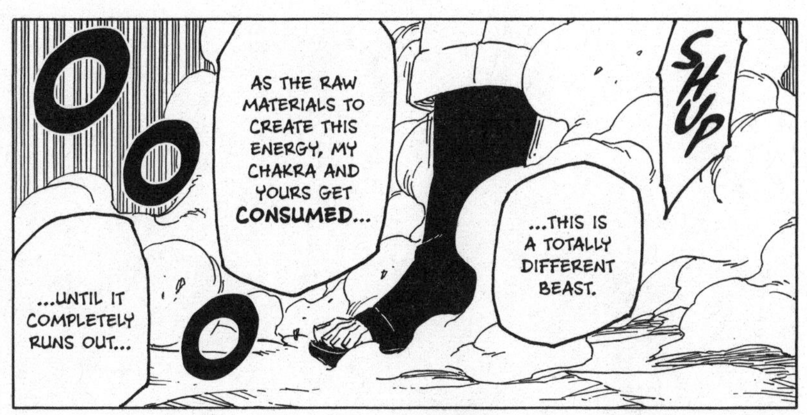

LISTEN, DON'T MAKE ANY UNNECESSARY MOVES.

EVEN RID YOURSELF OF SUPERFLUOUS THOUGHTS.

THOSE ARE THE TRICKS TO KEEP THIS **BARYON MODE** GOING FOR AS LONG AS POSSIBLE.

SHUP

WOOOOO

SHUP

ZZP
GAKK

ZSHH

!!

...

TA
K

ZWUSH
WSH

VOOSH
GAH!!
FWSH
QUIT DARTING AROU--

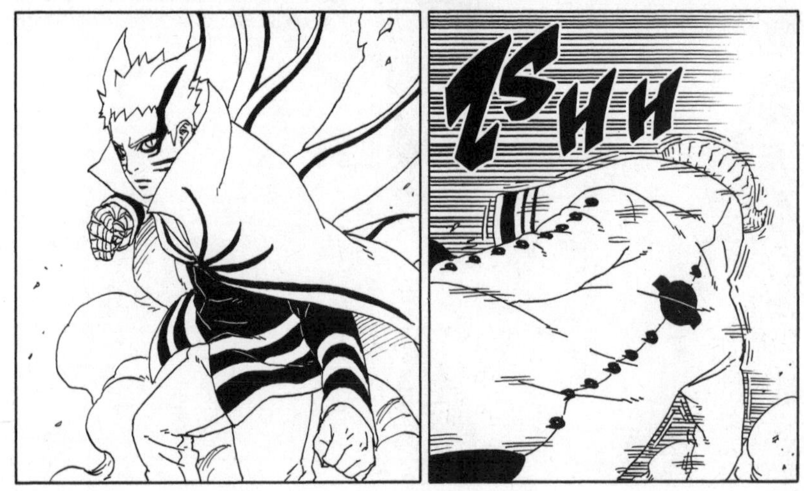
ZSHH

...

WOOO

UNBELIEVABLE.
THEY'RE EVEN... NO...
NARUTO'S ACTUALLY BEATING HIM!

...
SHK
EEN

VOOSH

BAM

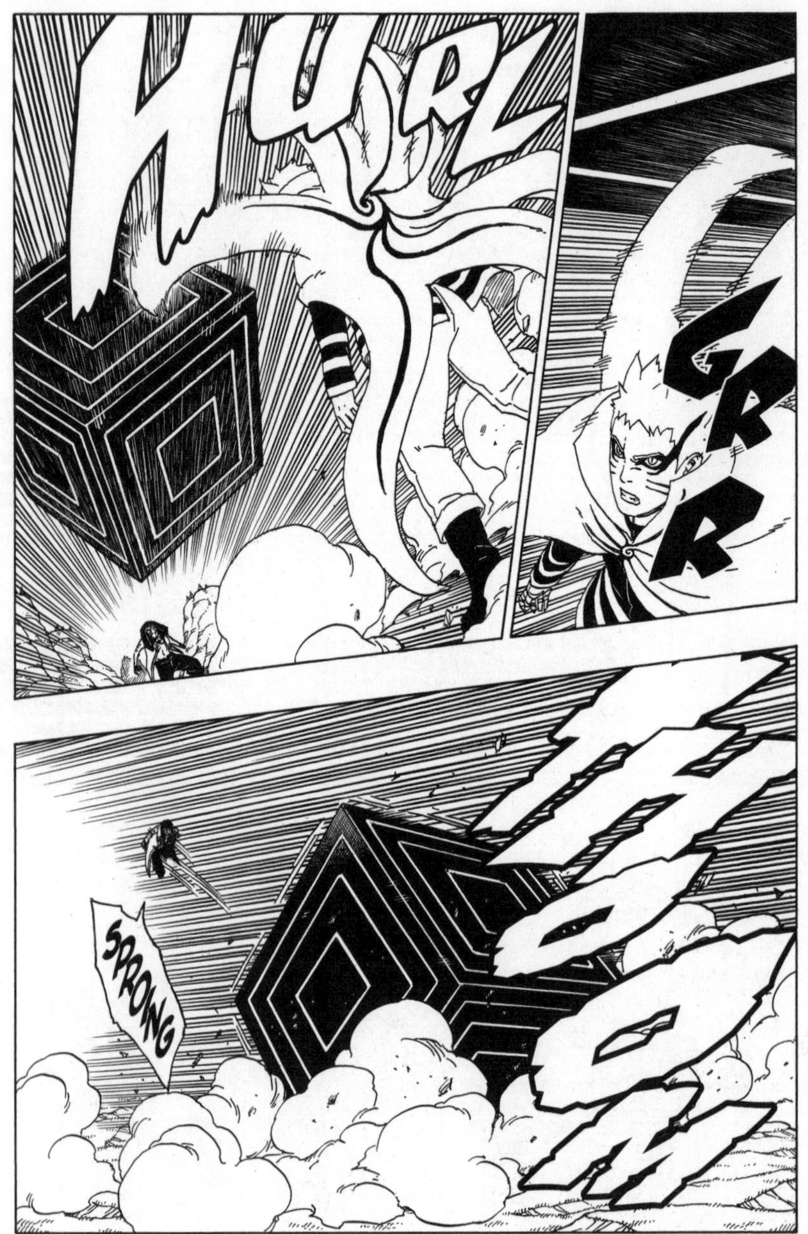
HURL
GRRR
SPROING
THOOM

THWAK

!

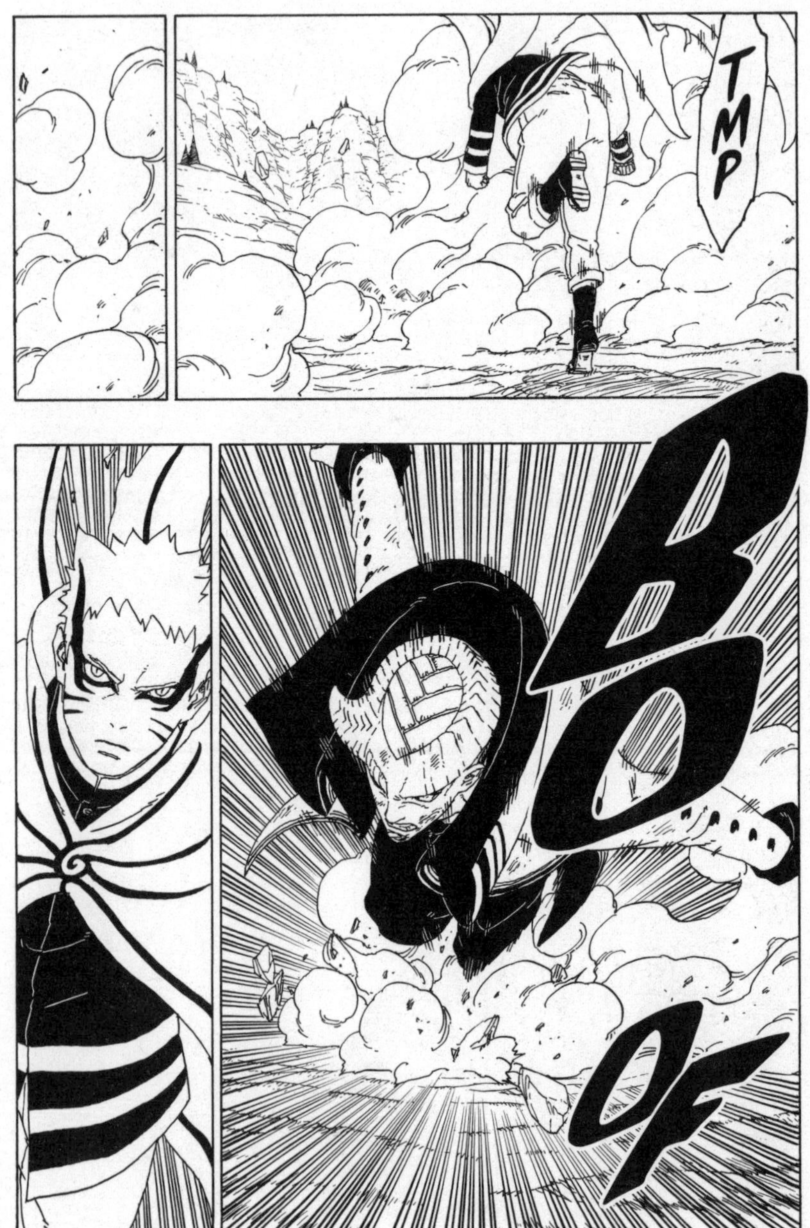
TMP
BOOF

BAM

WHAM

THWAK

ZSHH

TMP

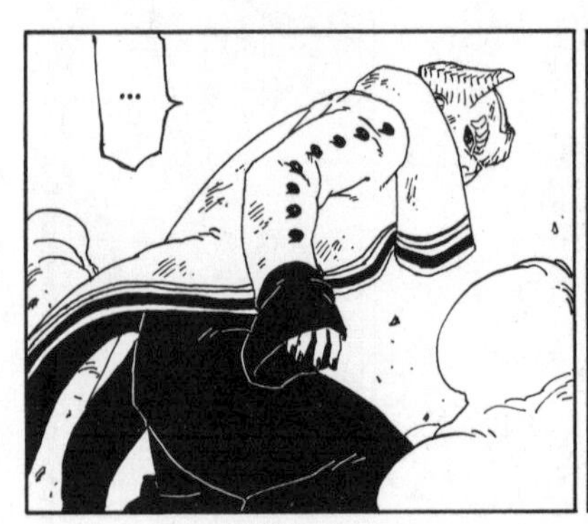
...

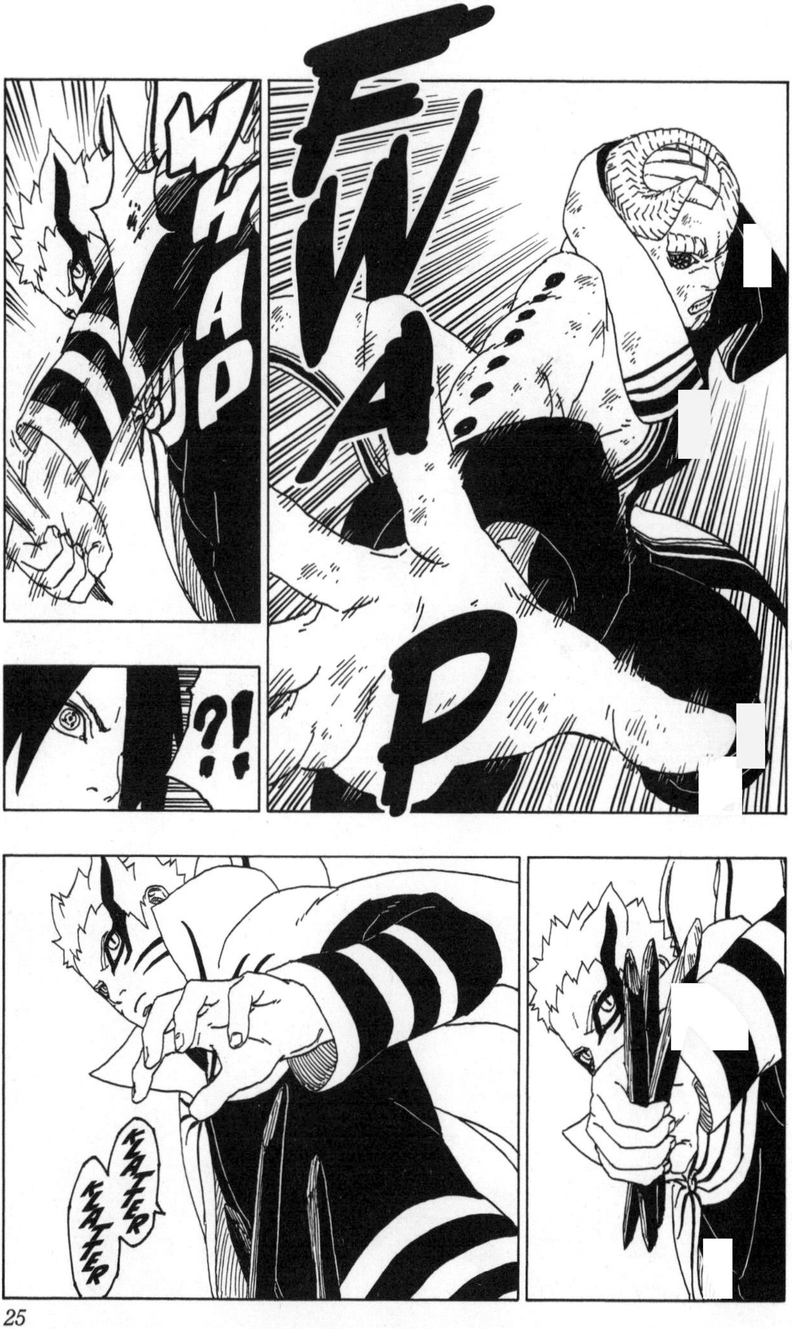

WHAP

HE STOPPED THOSE HIGH-SPEED RODS!
UNBELIEVABLE! I'M BARELY ABLE TO EVEN TRACK THEM WITH MY SHARINGAN!

NO WAY!
IMPOSSIBLE! HOW DID HE POWER UP SO DRASTICALLY, SO FAST?!

FWOOO

THAT PROSTHETIC HAND... IT RUNS ON CHAKRA, RIGHT?
IT'S USUALLY PRETTY HARD TO FIND A COMPATIBLE MATCH. YOU'RE LUCKY.

...

THAT WAS ORIGINALLY CREATED FOR LORD SEVENTH'S USE.
SO IT ONLY RESPONDS TO ***HIS*** CHAKRA.
WHAT?

...

LORD SEVENTH HAS BEEN SHARING SOME OF HIS CHAKRA WITH KAWAKI...
HE'S ESSENTIALLY CONSTANTLY KNEADING CHAKRA.
...SO THAT THE HAND FUNCTIONS AT ALL TIMES.
...
THAT'S UNEXPECTED.
IS THERE NO END TO HIS GENEROSITY?
...

UM...
ARE YOU...
...ABLE TO RESTORE HIS RIGHT HAND, MISTER AMADO?
YES, OF COURSE.
IT'LL BE MY FIRST TASK WHEN THIS IS ALL OVER.
HE'S DUE FOR A CHECK-UP ANYWAY.
...
GLEAM

...
IT'S...

LORD SEVENTH'S CHAKRA...
IT'S WEAKEN-ING!!

WOOOOOO

UNH...

DNK

?!

B-BBFFF

HUFF

HUFF

...!
G-
G-
DAD!!

WHAT'S GOING ON?!
HIS CHAKRA... IT'S DROPPING RAPIDLY!

THROB
OW!

UGH... I HURT ALL OVER!
DAMMIT! I CAN'T...
...STAY AWAKE...

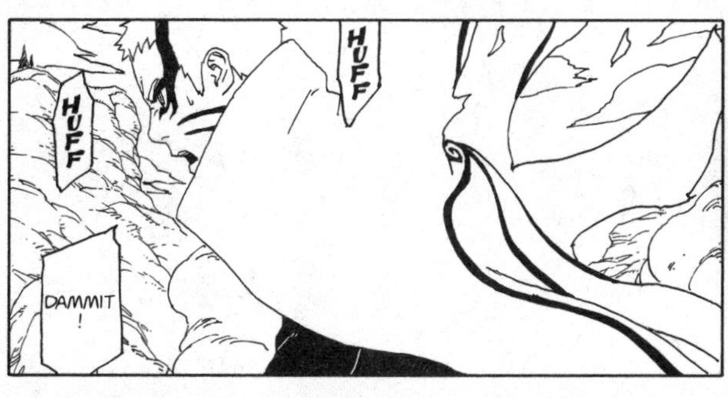
HUFF
HUFF
DAMMIT!

THE ENERGY COST IS STEEPER THAN I EXPECTED.
I DON'T THINK I'VE GOT MUCH TIME LEFT...

...
I SEE.

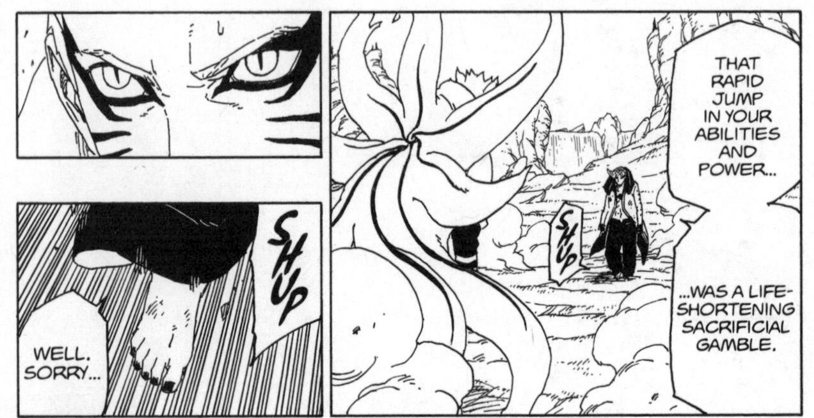

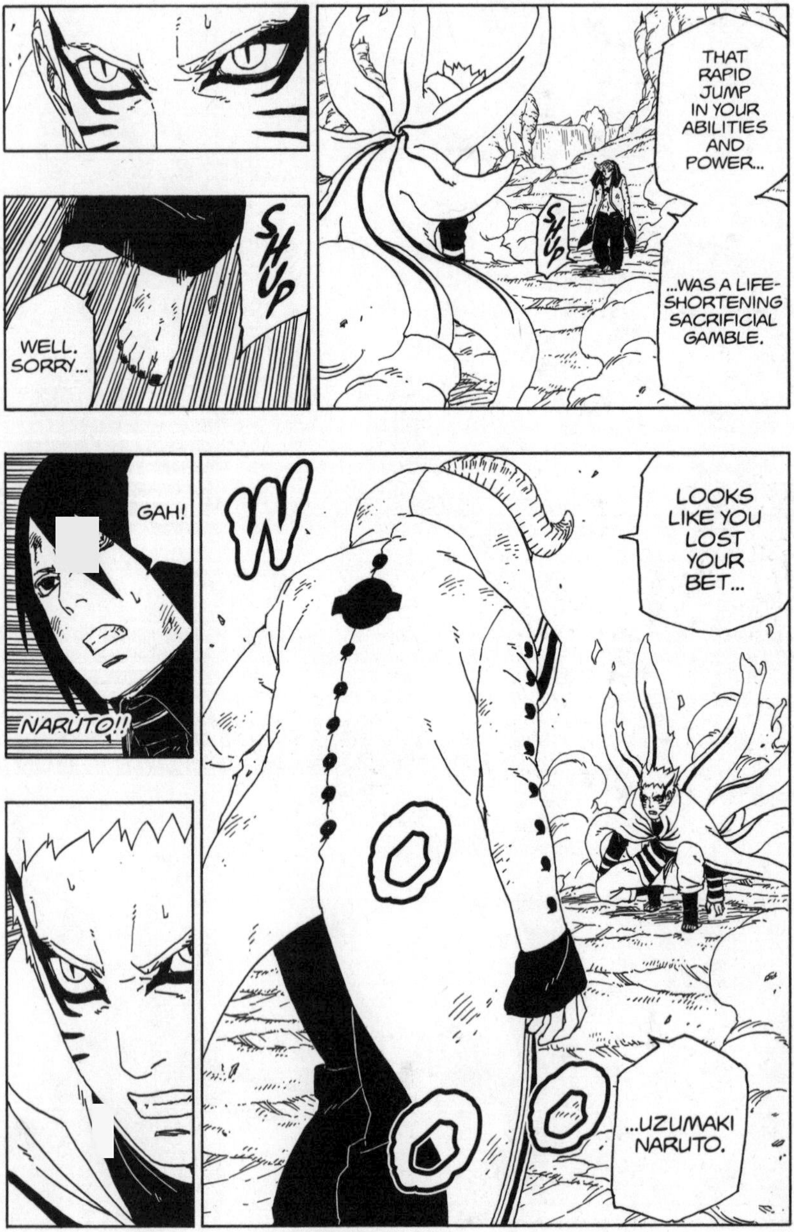

THAT RAPID JUMP IN YOUR ABILITIES AND POWER...
SHUP
...WAS A LIFE-SHORTENING SACRIFICIAL GAMBLE.
SHUP
WELL. SORRY...
W
LOOKS LIKE YOU LOST YOUR BET...
...UZUMAKI NARUTO.
GAH!
NARUTO!!

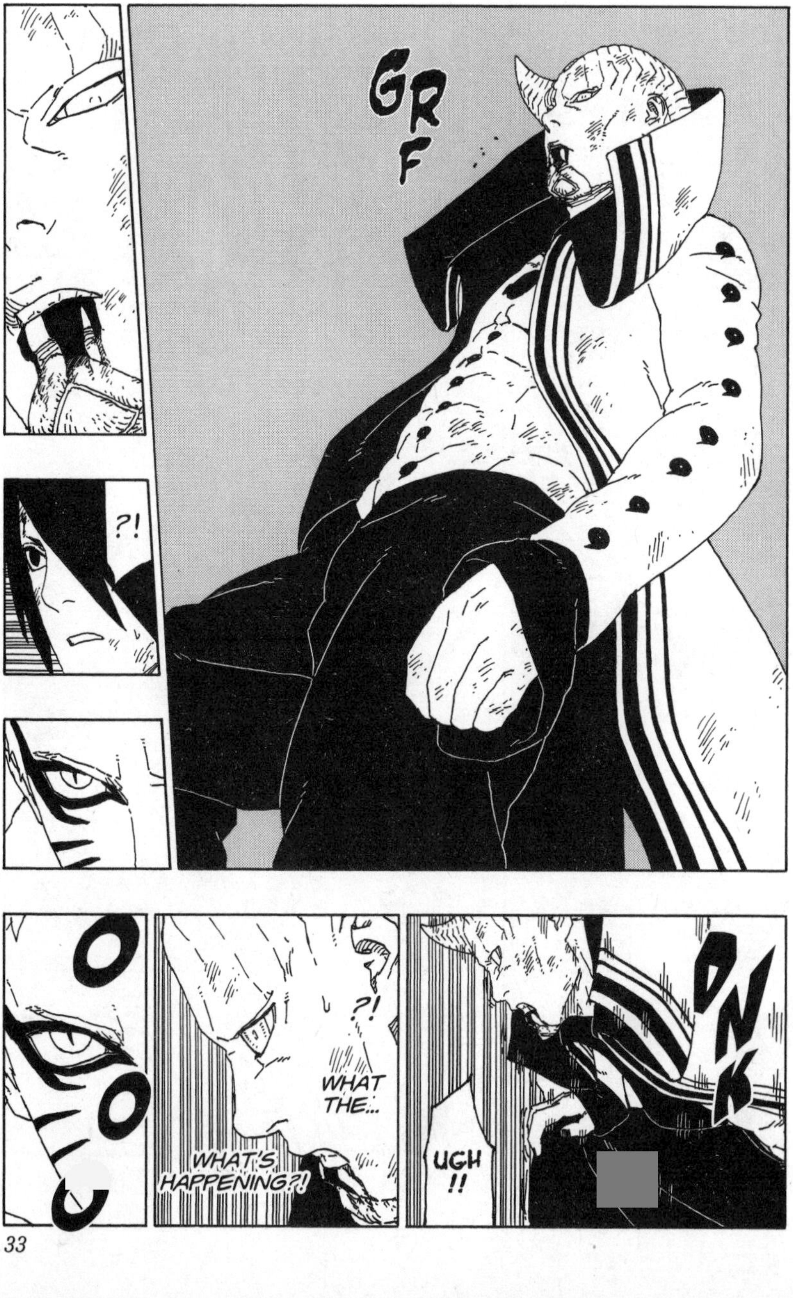

GRF

?!

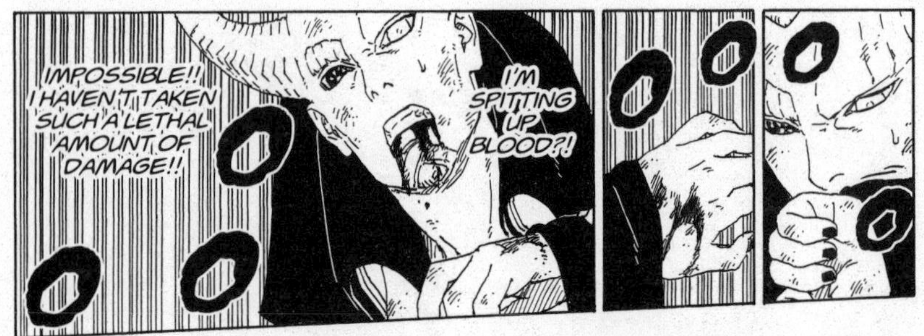

HOKAGE, YOU--!!

WHAT HAVE YOU DONE?!!

HEH.

NOW BEGINS THE REAL GAME!

TO SEE...

...WHICH OF US DIES FIRST!!

!

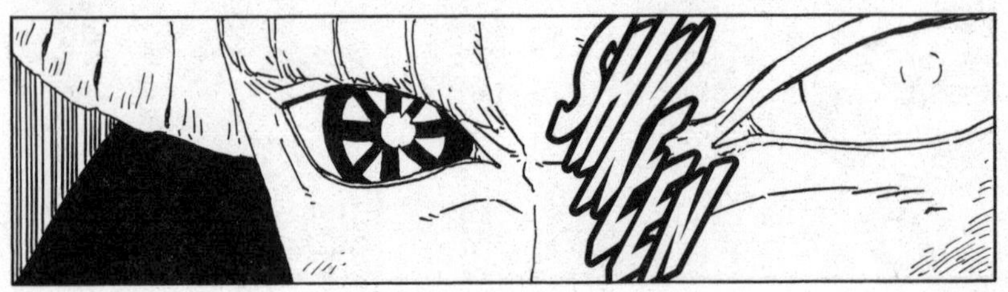

B-BFFF...

BFFF

!!

NO...

DON'T TELL ME...!!!!

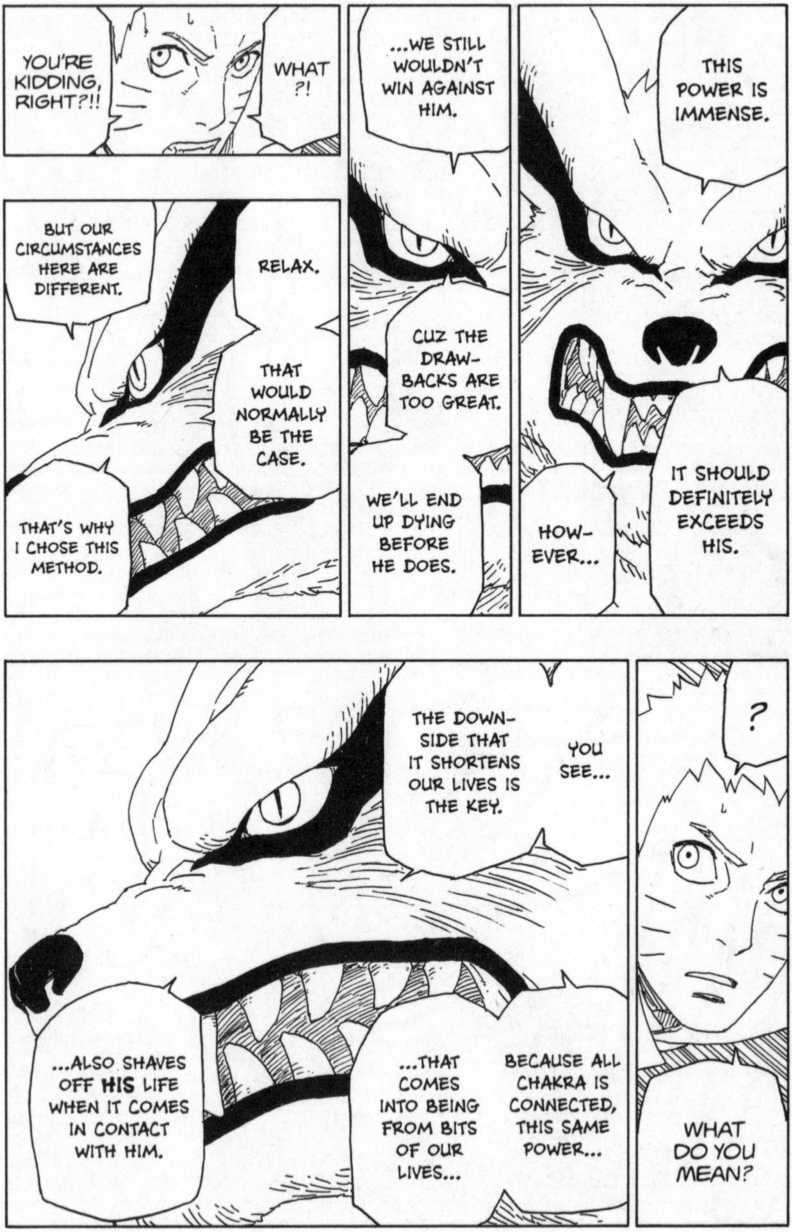

THIS POWER IS IMMENSE.
IT SHOULD DEFINITELY EXCEEDS HIS.
HOW-EVER...
...WE STILL WOULDN'T WIN AGAINST HIM.
CUZ THE DRAW-BACKS ARE TOO GREAT.
WE'LL END UP DYING BEFORE HE DOES.
WHAT ?!
YOU'RE KIDDING, RIGHT?!!
RELAX.
THAT WOULD NORMALLY BE THE CASE.
BUT OUR CIRCUMSTANCES HERE ARE DIFFERENT.
THAT'S WHY I CHOSE THIS METHOD.
?
WHAT DO YOU MEAN?
YOU SEE...
THE DOWN-SIDE THAT IT SHORTENS OUR LIVES IS THE KEY.
BECAUSE ALL CHAKRA IS CONNECTED, THIS SAME POWER...
...THAT COMES INTO BEING FROM BITS OF OUR LIVES...
...ALSO SHAVES OFF **HIS** LIFE WHEN IT COMES IN CONTACT WITH HIM.

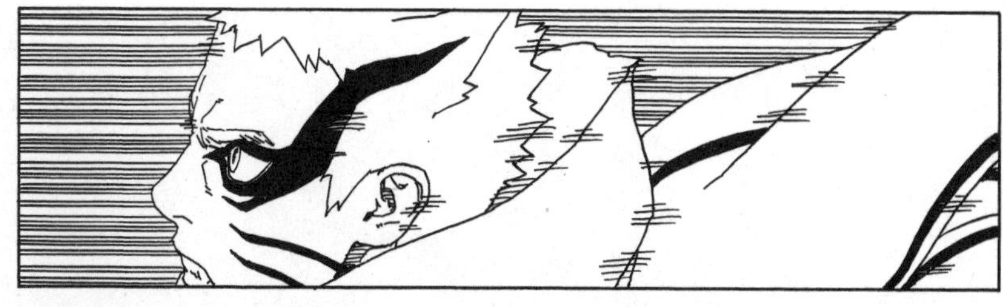

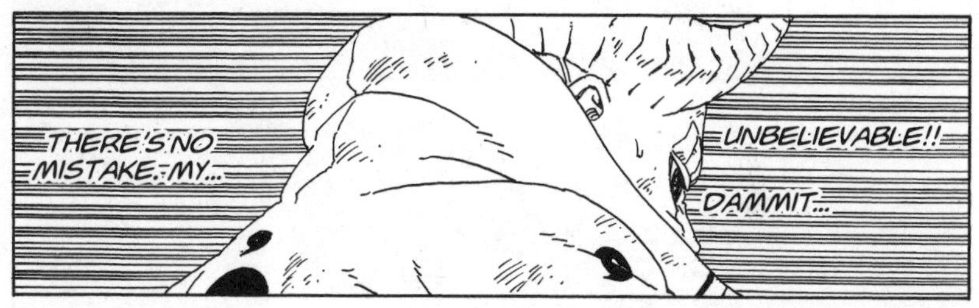

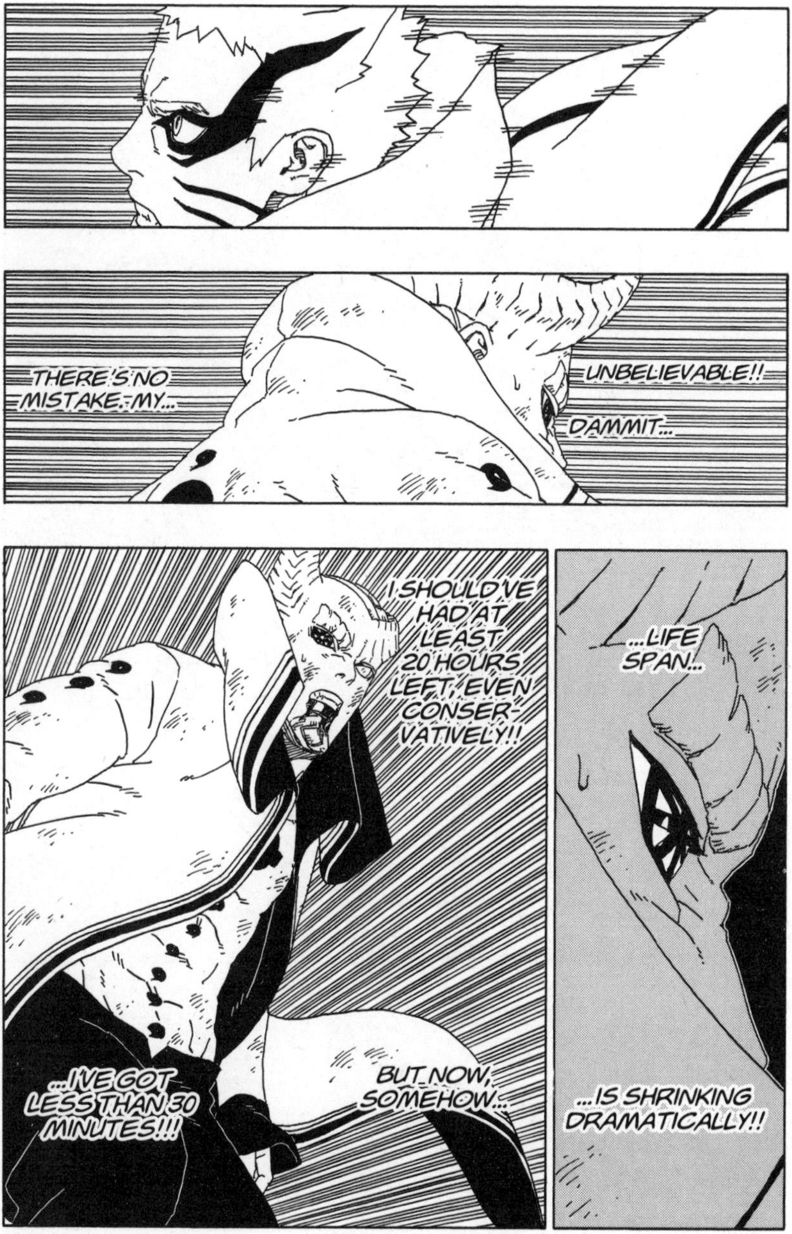

...LIFE SPAN...

...IS SHRINKING DRAMATICALLY!!

I SHOULD'VE HAD AT LEAST 20 HOURS LEFT, EVEN CONSERVATIVELY!!

BUT NOW, SOMEHOW...

...I'VE GOT LESS THAN 30 MINUTES!!!

LISTEN.
DON'T THINK ABOUT TAKING HIM DOWN.
FOCUS ONLY ON...
...GETTING IN YOUR ATTACKS.
JUST LIKE A BOXER AIMING TO WIN BY DECISION.
THK
SHAVE OFF THE REST OF HIS LIFE...
...BEFORE OURS RUNS OUT!

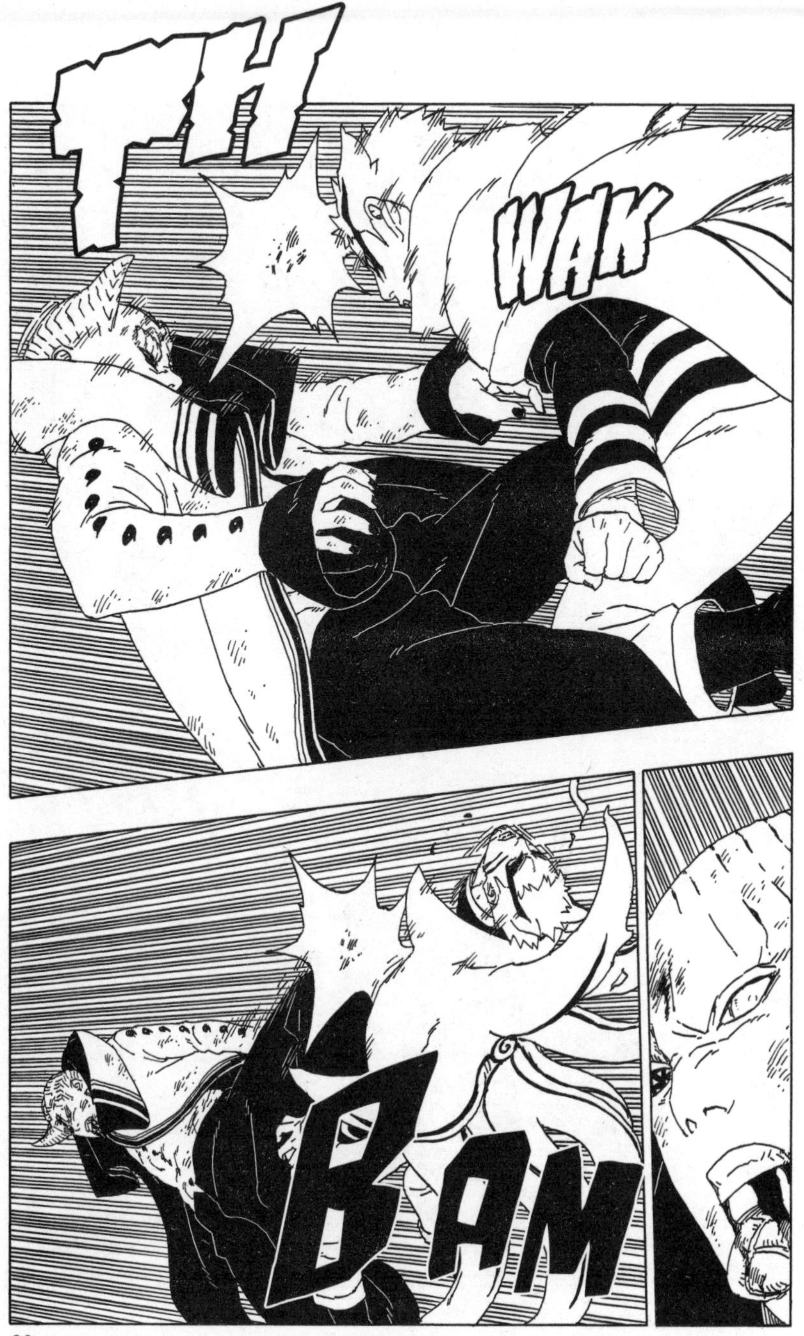
TH
WAK
BAM

WSH
ZWISH
FWSH
BLAM

DMP

THDTHD

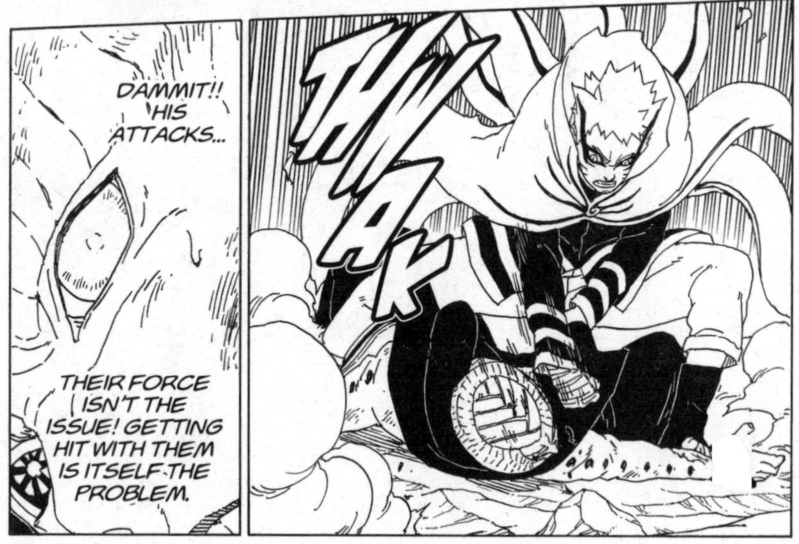
THWAK
DAMMIT!! HIS ATTACKS...
THEIR FORCE ISN'T THE ISSUE! GETTING HIT WITH THEM IS ITSELF THE PROBLEM.

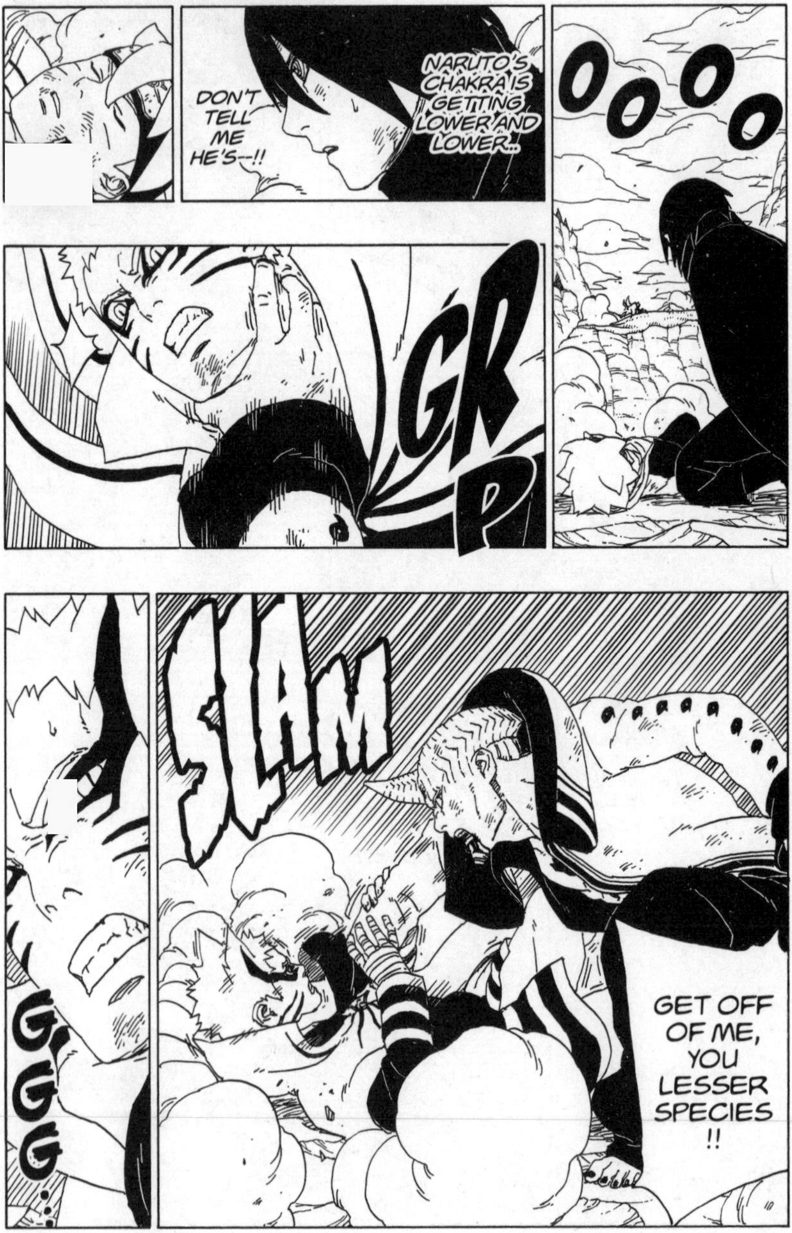

OOOOO

NARUTO'S CHAKRA IS GETTING LOWER AND LOWER...

DON'T TELL ME HE'S--!!

GRIP

SLAM

GET OFF OF ME, YOU LESSER SPECIES!!

GGG...

FLICKER
FLICKER

BFF

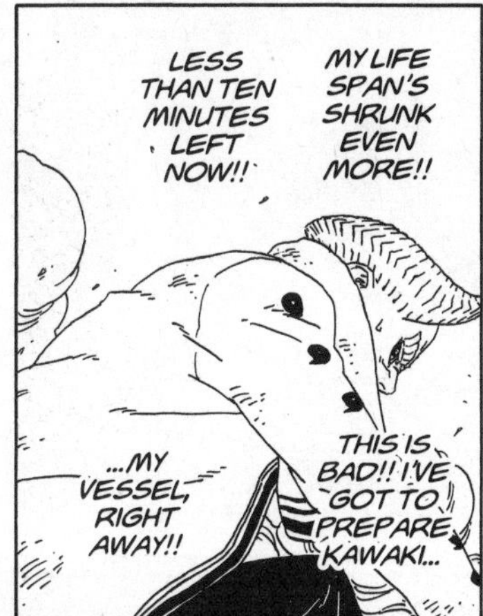
MY LIFE SPAN'S SHRUNK EVEN MORE!!
LESS THAN TEN MINUTES LEFT NOW!!
THIS IS BAD!! I'VE GOT TO PREPARE KAWAKI...
...MY VESSEL, RIGHT AWAY!!

HEH HEH.
IT'S TOO LATE NOW.
BOO-HOO TO YOU.

SQUEEZE
HAKK
ARGH !!

SHUT UP, YOU WORM!!
GGG...

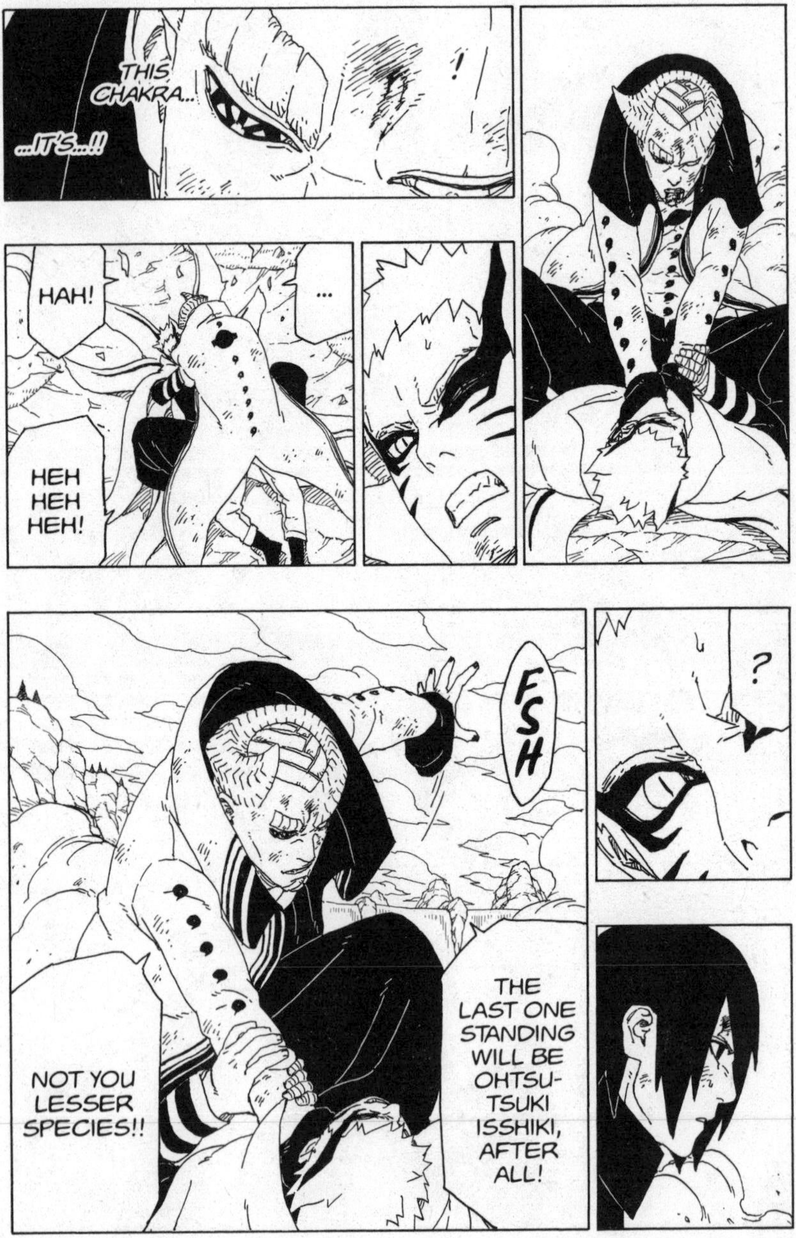

!

THIS CHAKRA...

...IT'S...!!

...

HAH!

HEH HEH HEH!

?

FSH

THE LAST ONE STANDING WILL BE OHTSUTSUKI ISSHIKI, AFTER ALL!

NOT YOU LESSER SPECIES!!

FWOOOO

OWW!
EXPLAIN, KAWAKI!!
IS NARUTO ALL RIGHT?!

HOW THE HECK SHOULD I KNOW?!!
SHADDUP AND LET ME FOCUS!!

ZWW

ZWOOSH

!

WHA?!

?!
HUH
?!
...!
NO
WAY!

THUD

I SEE. SO THAT UNSIGHTLY RIGHT HAND...

...WAS FUNCTIONING VIA ***YOUR*** CHAKRA, HOKAGE.

I'M GRATEFUL TO YOU. THANKS TO THAT MEDDLE-SOME LINK...

...I WAS ABLE TO DETECT KAWAKI AND DRAG HIM OUT HERE, AT THIS LATE MOMENT.

BLINK

WHAT?! NO WAY!!!

THIS IS BAD!!!

Number 53:
That's Reality

HELLO THERE, KAWAKI.
WE FINALLY MEET AGAIN.

WHAT HAPPENED?!
KAWAKI SUDDENLY DISAPPEARED!

C-COULD IT HAVE BEEN ISSHIKI'S DOING?
BUT WITHOUT KARMA, HOW WOULD HE...?

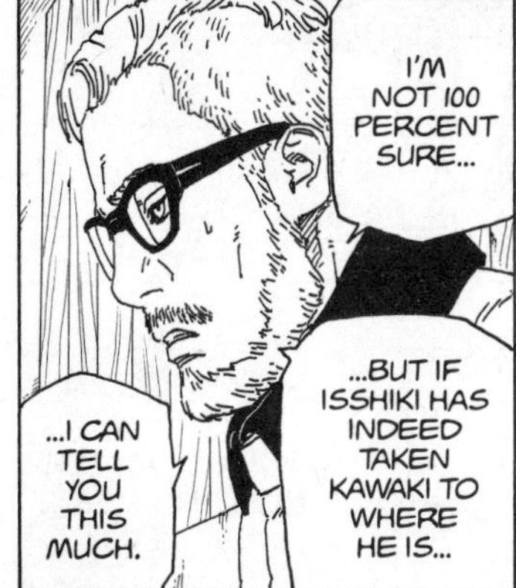
I'M NOT 100 PERCENT SURE...
...BUT IF ISSHIKI HAS INDEED TAKEN KAWAKI TO WHERE HE IS...
...I CAN TELL YOU THIS MUCH.

WE'RE OUT OF OPTIONS.
WE'RE COMPLETELY...
...DONE FOR.

VWOOOOO

SO THIS IS HIM...
OHTSUTSUKI ISSHIKI!
AND HE...

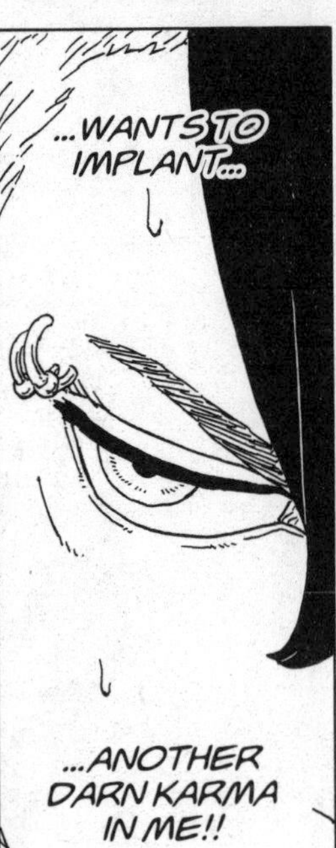
...WANTS TO IMPLANT...
...ANOTHER DARN KARMA IN ME!!

KAWAKI!

THAT WAS A CLOSE CALL.
I SENSE I ONLY HAVE FIVE MINUTES OF LIFE LEFT.
I CAN'T BELIEVE THESE FAILURES MANAGED TO DRIVE ME INTO SUCH A CORNER.

...

SO IF WE CAN...
...AVOID HIM IMPLANTING YOU WITH ANOTHER KARMA BEFORE HIS LIFE RUNS OUT...
WE WIN.

EVEN A MONSTER CAN'T ESCAPE DEATH.

HEH.
ONLY FIVE MINUTES, HUH?
I'M JUMPING FOR JOY THAT I GET TO WITNESS YOUR WORTHLESS LIFE ENDING FOR GOOD!

HMPH. IT'S NOTHING FANCY.
NO MORE THAN A SLIGHTLY LENGTHY NAP.
AND THEN I'LL RESURRECT ONCE IT'S TIME.
WITH YOUR BODY, WHICH IS ABOUT TO REGAIN KARMA...
...AS MY NEW VESSEL.

DAMMIT!

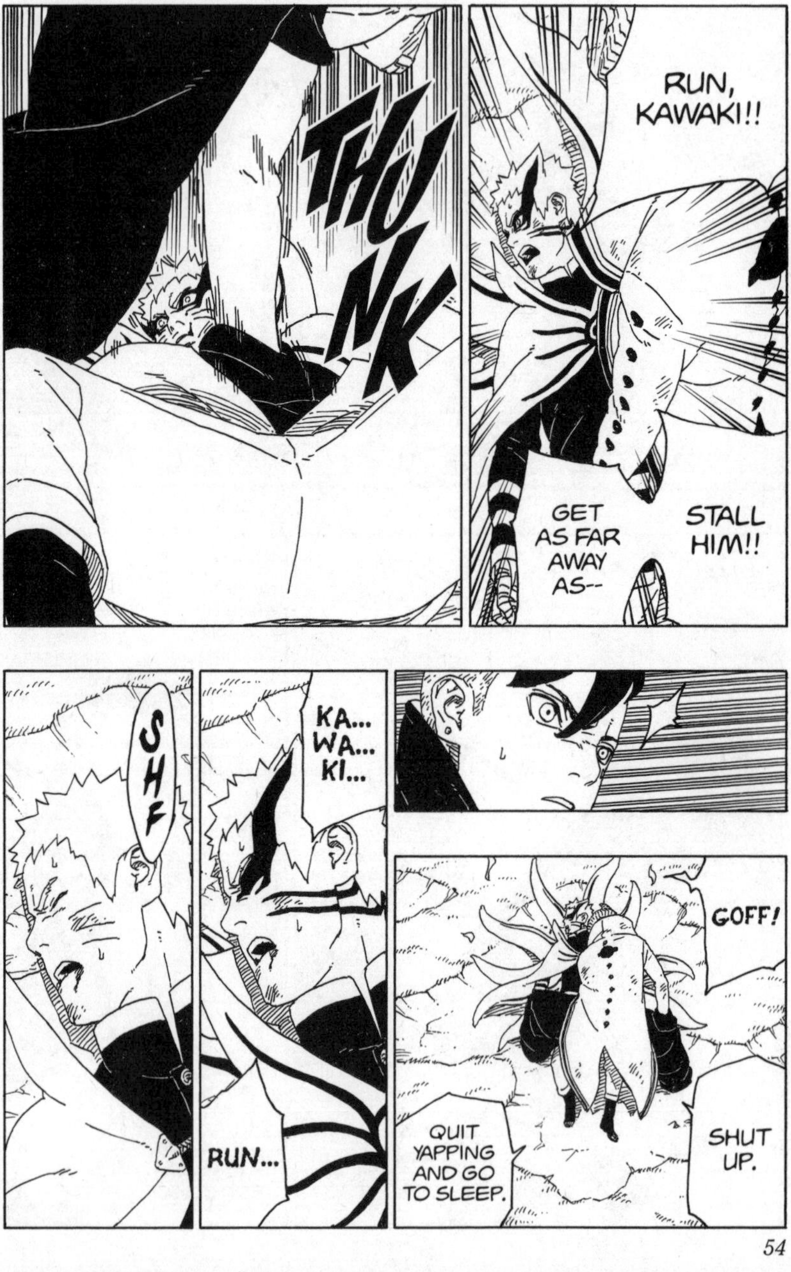

RUN, KAWAKI!!

STALL HIM!!

GET AS FAR AWAY AS--

THUNK

GOFF!

SHUT UP.

QUIT YAPPING AND GO TO SLEEP.

KA... WA... KI...

RUN...

SHF

HEY, NOW.

ZP!

YOU KNOW YOU CAN'T ESCAPE.

GRP

UGH!
GUH...

DON'T STRUGGLE.
IT'LL BE OVER IN A FLASH.

WHEEOOOO
EEEN

VWOOOOO
HAK HAK
WEEZ

!
WHAT ?!

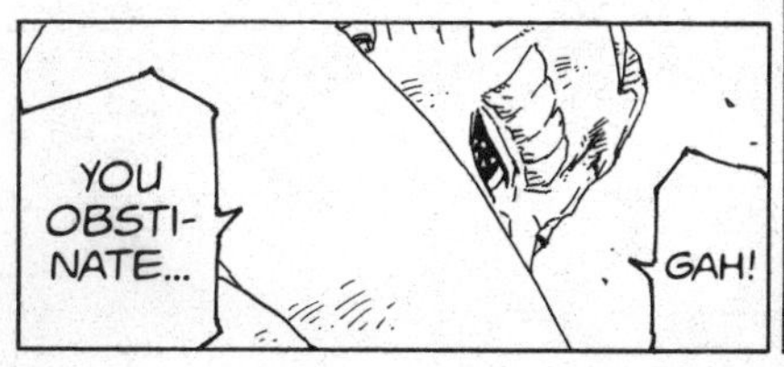
GAH!
YOU OBSTI-NATE...

KAWAKI !!
PICK THAT UP...
...AND THROW IT AT YOUR FEET!

!

FWIP

BOOF

KVOOOOSH

GAH!
WORTH-LESS TRICKS!!

THWAK

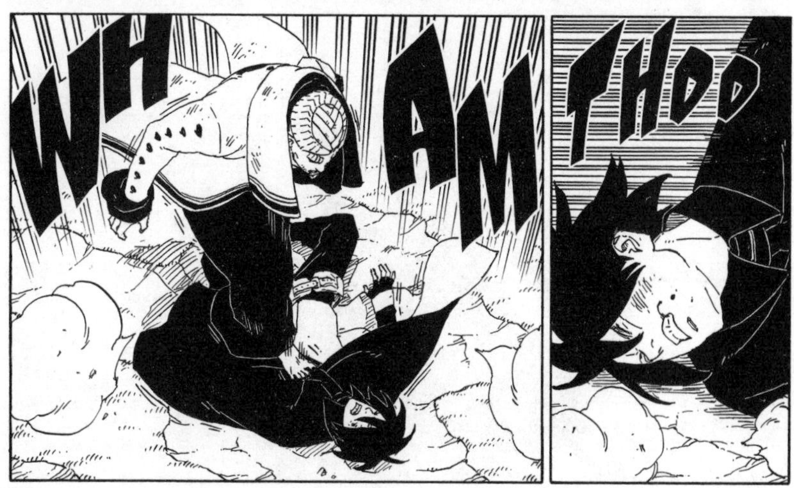
THOD
WHAM

KAWAKI... JUST KEEP YOUR DISTANCE FROM HIM!

HUFF

HUFF

FOOLS !!

A SMOKE SCREEN WON'T TRICK THE BYAKUGAN!

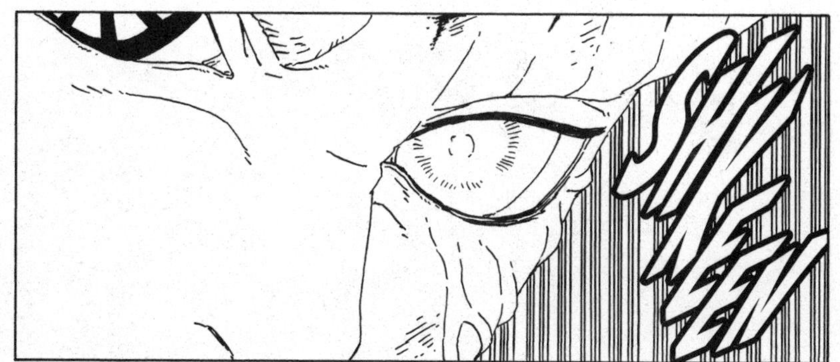
SHWEEN

OOOOO

?!

VWOOO

YOU'RE THE FOOL.
IT'S A MINERAL DUST THAT OBSTRUCTS CLAIRVOYANT POWERS. IT ONLY LASTS A FEW MINUTES...
...BUT THAT'S ALL WE NEED!

GWOOOOO...

WHAT'S GOING ON?!!

HUH?!

OOOOO

OO

GRIK

!

TAK

KAAAAWAAAAKII!!

BZZP

BZP

G-WOOO

VWOOOOO
HUFF
HUFF

WHRL
HUFF

HOW DARE YOU?!
I WON'T LET YOU ESCAPE!!!

NICE! NOW PLEASE...
...JUST KEEP ON RUNNING AND GET AWAY!!

HUFF
HUFF

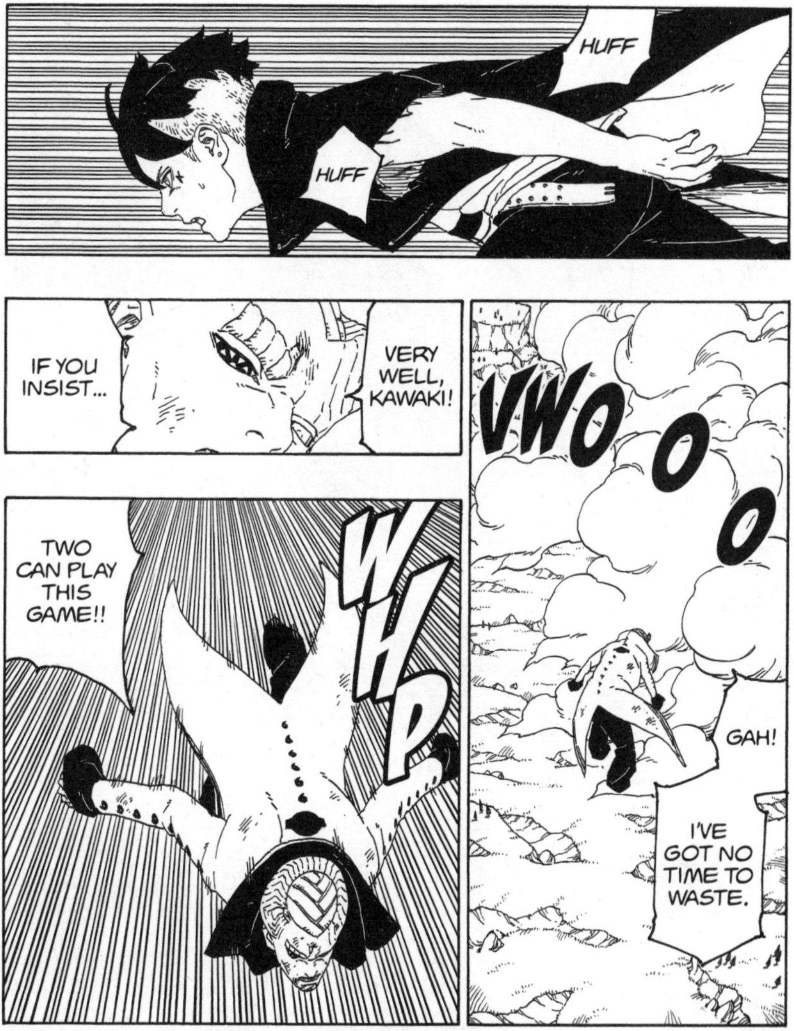

VWOOOO
GAH!
I'VE GOT NO TIME TO WASTE.
VERY WELL, KAWAKI!
IF YOU INSIST...
WHP
TWO CAN PLAY THIS GAME!!

GOFF!!

WHAMM

ARE YOU LISTENING, KAWAKI?!!!

SHOW YOURSELF WITHIN 20 SECONDS!!! OR ELSE...

...I'LL RIP HIS CHEST OPEN AND KILL HIM!!!

!

RUN ALL YOU WANT, AS LONG AS...

...YOU DON'T CARE THAT YOUR BELOVED HOKAGE WILL DIE!!

DAMMIT...

YOU BASTARD!!

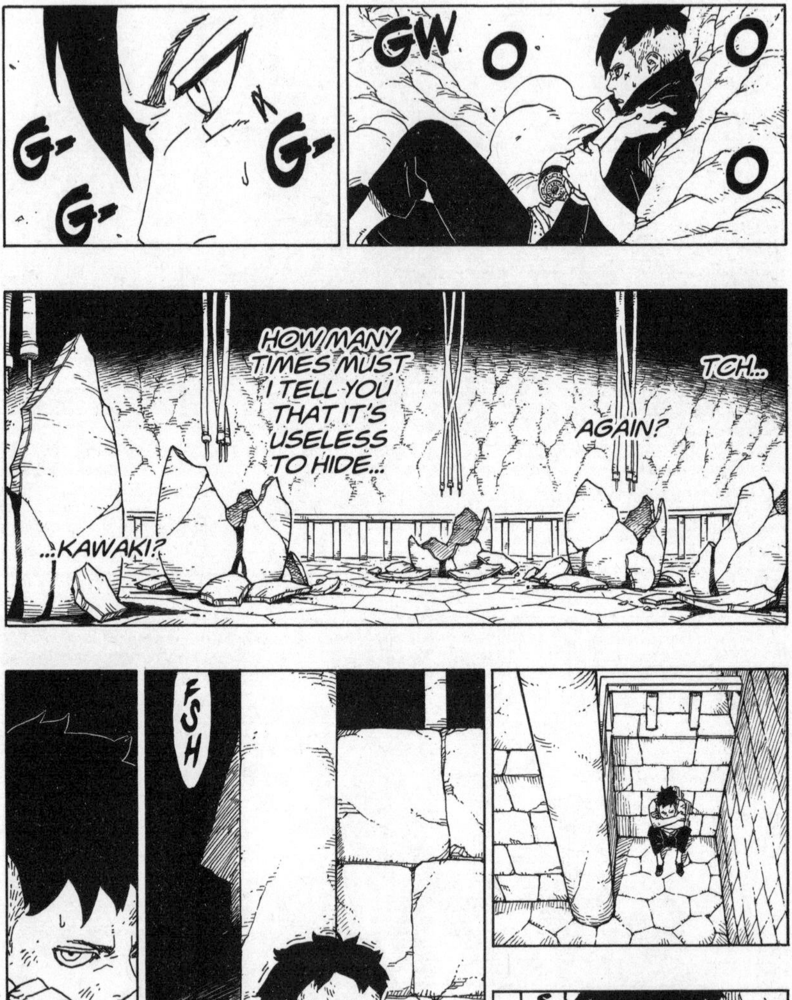

SHDD

SHDD

FSH

JRK

...

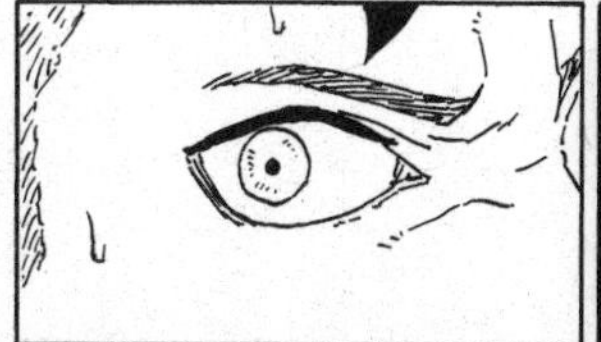

PREPARE TO BE PUNISHED...
...KAWAKI...

HUFF
HUFF

GRP

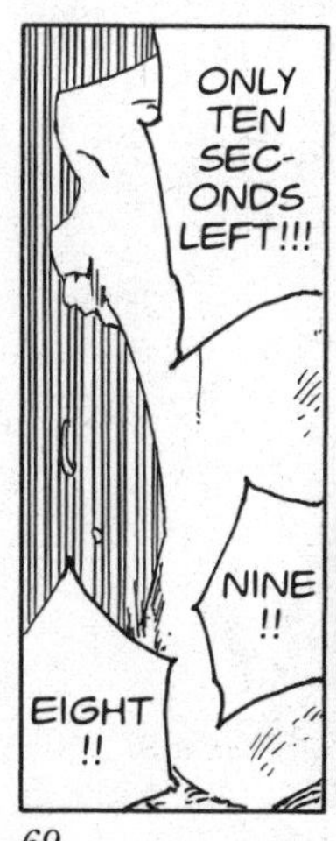
ONLY TEN SEC-ONDS LEFT!!!
NINE!!
EIGHT!!

LET'S JUST SAY...

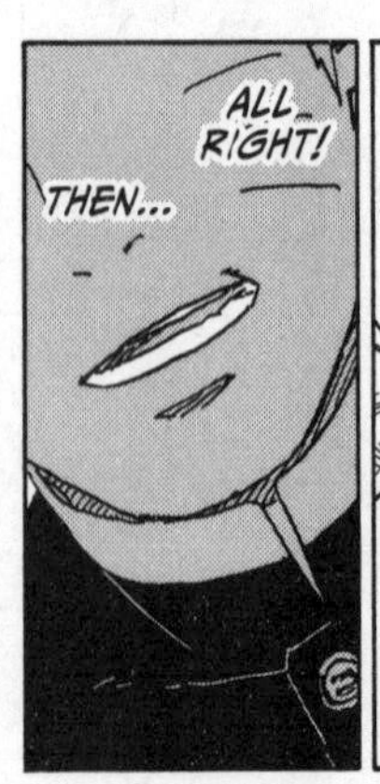

YOU'RE MY STUDENT...

...STARTING TODAY!

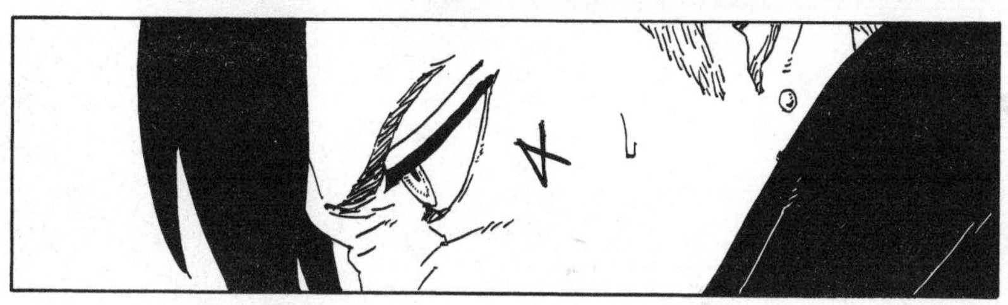

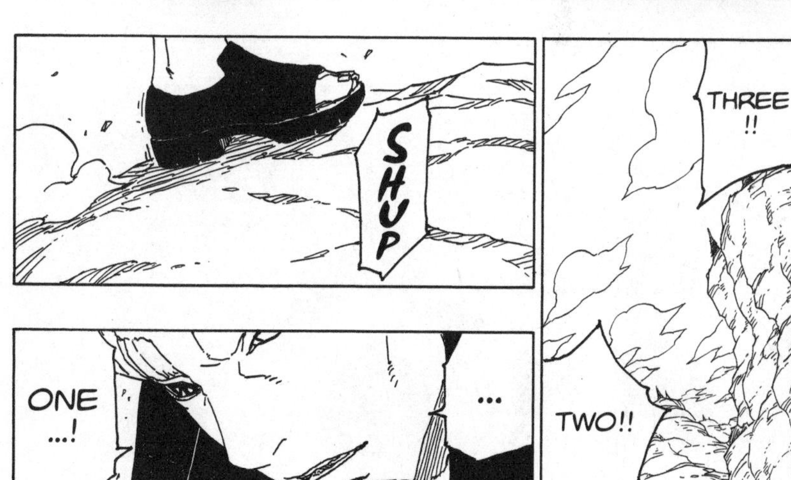

VWOOO
KA-
WA-
KI...
!
THAT
IDIOT
!!

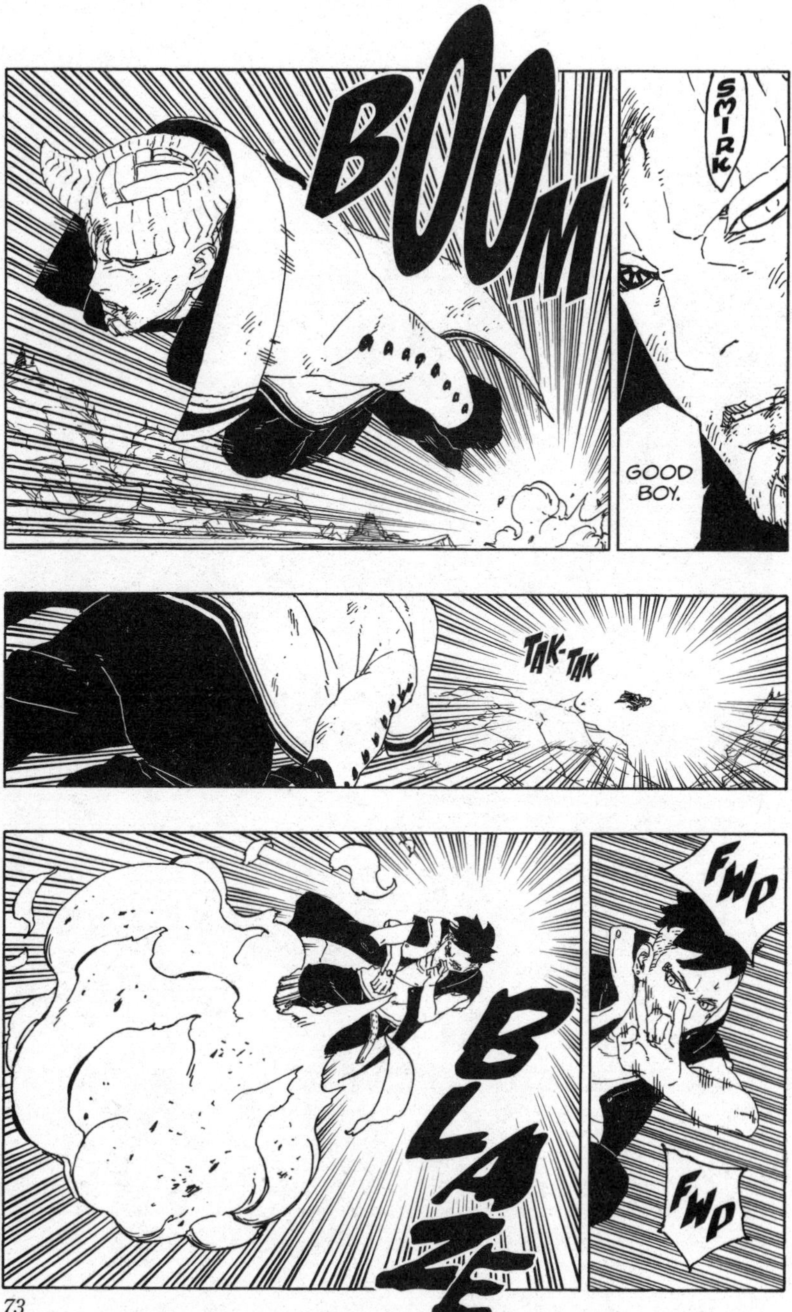

SMIRK
GOOD BOY.
BOOM

NIN-
JUTSU
?!
BAH.

BZIP

GRP

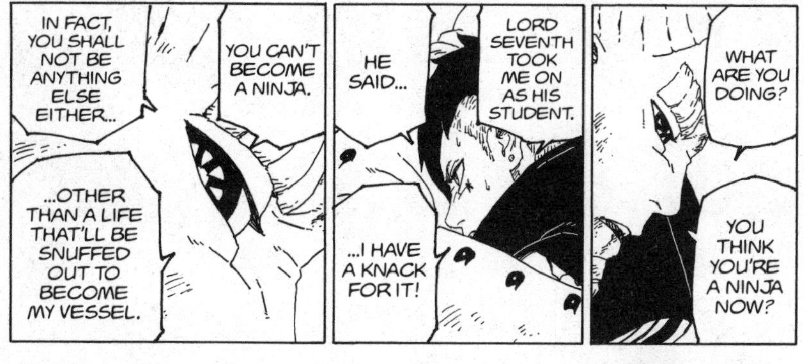
WHAT ARE YOU DOING?
YOU THINK YOU'RE A NINJA NOW?
LORD SEVENTH TOOK ME ON AS HIS STUDENT.
HE SAID...
...I HAVE A KNACK FOR IT!
YOU CAN'T BECOME A NINJA.
IN FACT, YOU SHALL NOT BE ANYTHING ELSE EITHER...
...OTHER THAN A LIFE THAT'LL BE SNUFFED OUT TO BECOME MY VESSEL.

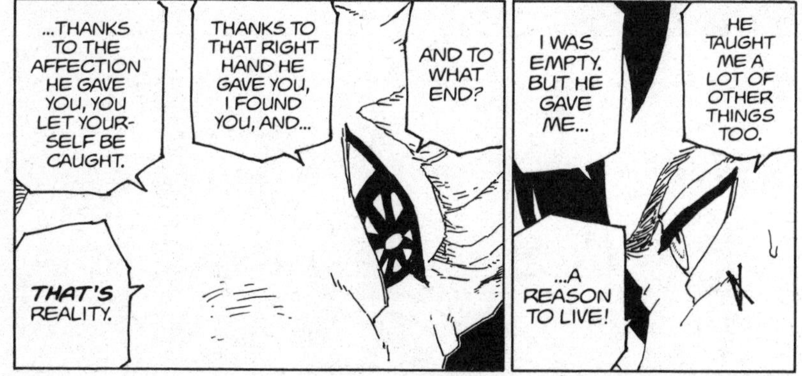
HE TAUGHT ME A LOT OF OTHER THINGS TOO.
I WAS EMPTY. BUT HE GAVE ME...
...A REASON TO LIVE!
AND TO WHAT END?
THANKS TO THAT RIGHT HAND HE GAVE YOU, I FOUND YOU, AND...
...THANKS TO THE AFFECTION HE GAVE YOU, YOU LET YOURSELF BE CAUGHT.
THAT'S REALITY.

HEH.

YOU DON'T UNDERSTAND A THING!

A WORLD WITHOUT LORD SEVENTH HAS NO WORTH TO ME.

I'D RATHER BE DEAD. THAT'S WHAT *I'M* SAYING!

GR
P

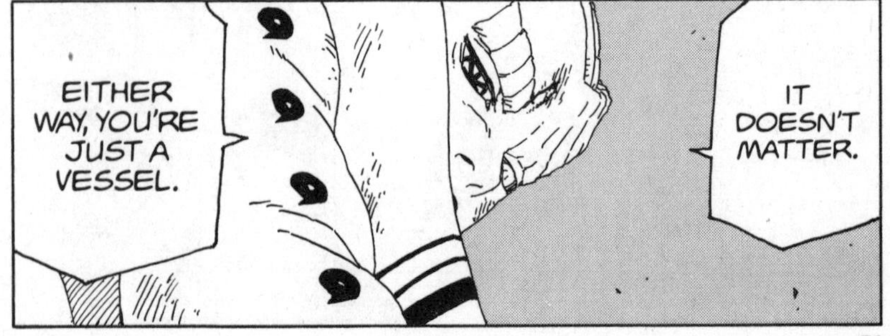

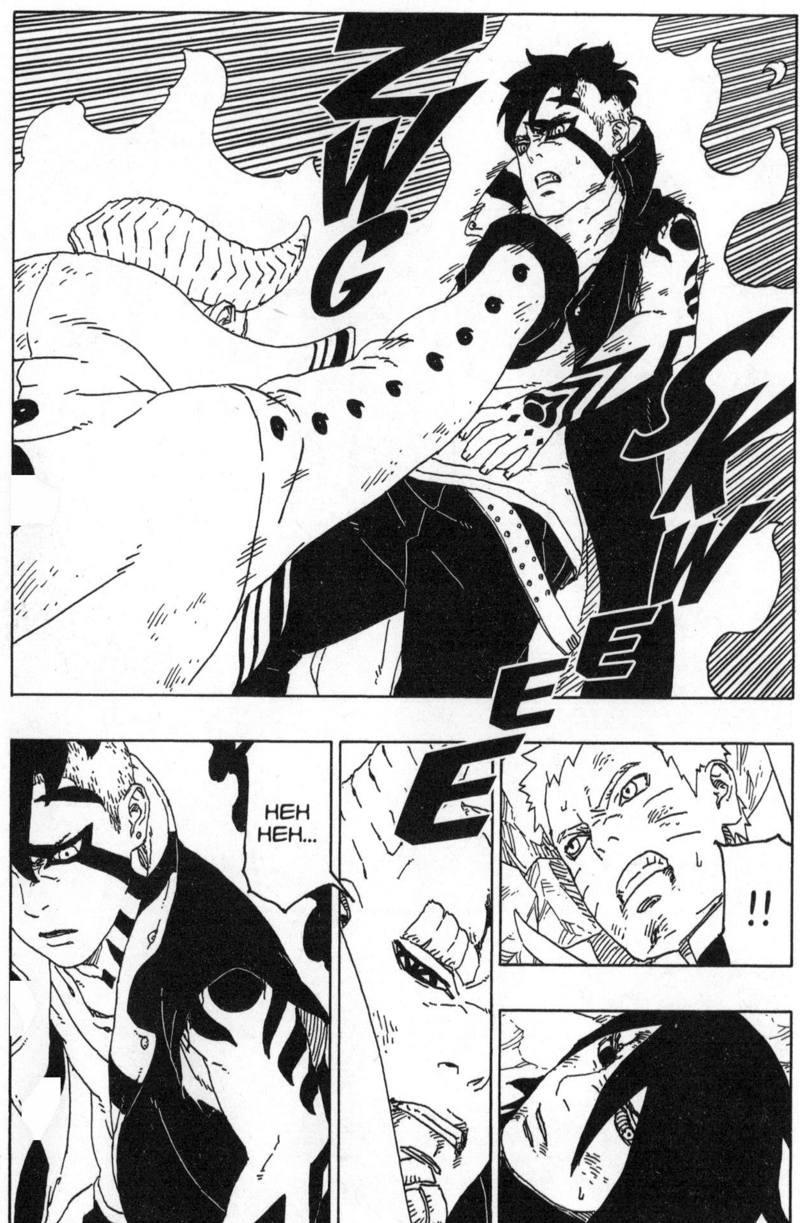
ZWG
SKWEEEE
HEH HEH...
!!

HA HA HA!

HA HA HA!!!

GW-

W-

W-

W-

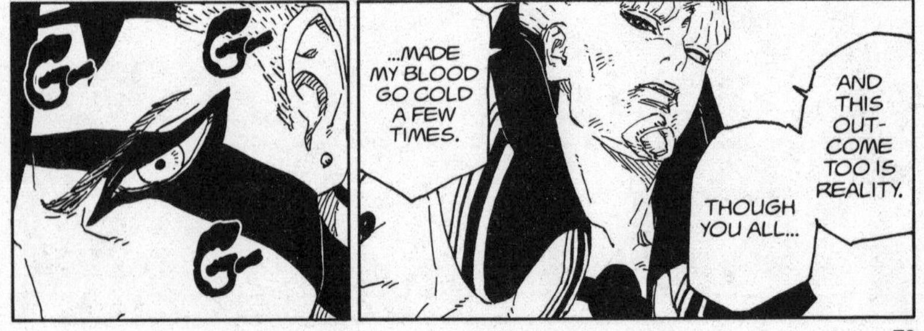

I CAN NOW GO TO SLEEP WORRY FREE.
HEH HEH HEH.

HA HA HA HA!!
DAMMIT !!!

DRB

OH...

DRB DRB
DRB

LOOKS LIKE MY LIFE'S RUN OUT.
YOU WERE SO CLOSE... HEH HEH.
I'LL GIVE YOU CREDIT FOR PUSHING ME THIS FAR DESPITE BEING A LESSER SPECIES...

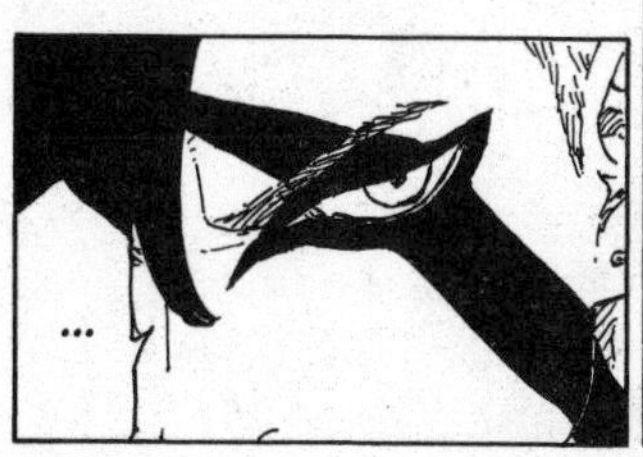
...

TSHHH

OWOOOOOO

?!

MIND TELLING US...

...HOW MUCH LONGER...

...YOU CAN CLING TO YOUR EXISTENCE? SECONDS?

HMM...

...MISTER OHTSU-TSUKI?

YOU!!!!

GRAB

WHAT HAVE YOU DONE?!!

DRBBB

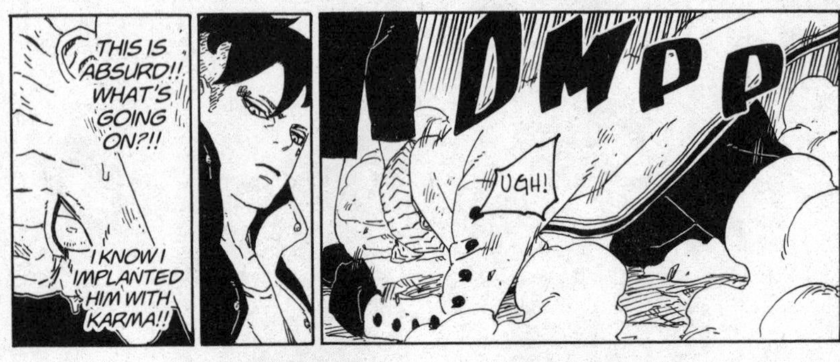
DMPP
UGH!
THIS IS ABSURD!! WHAT'S GOING ON?!!
I KNOW I IMPLANTED HIM WITH KARMA!!

SHUP

SHADOW DOPPEL-GANGER JUTSU.

BOOF

KA-WA-KI!

AH...

GAH...

SEEMS LIKE YOU WANNA SAY SOMETHING.

NOT THAT IT MATTERS.

SO WHATEVER IT IS...

THIS IS ***YOUR*** REALITY.

YOU'RE GONNA DIE, TOTALLY OUTSMARTED AND BEATEN BY A MERE VESSEL.

YOU...

...BAS...

...TARD...

DRB DRB

SMSH
TAK

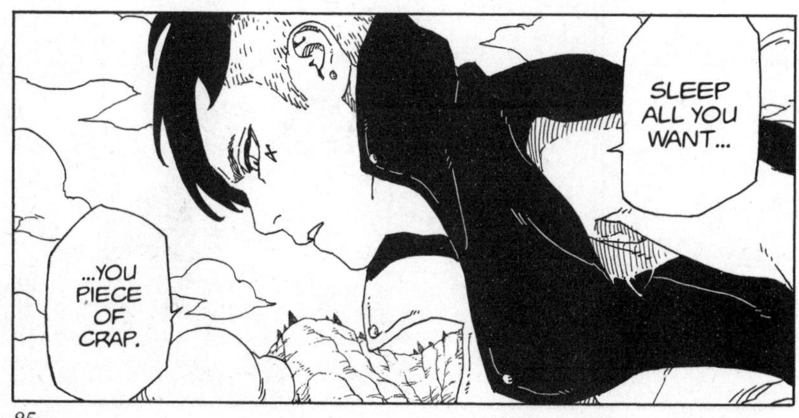

WHAT A SHOCKER!
A SHADOW DOPPEL-GANGER?!
IT'S STILL A WORK IN PROGRESS...
SHUP
I CAN BARELY MAKE THE ONE.
I'M GLAD IT WORKED.

ARE YOU OKAY...
...NARUTO?
SASUKE...
WHAT ABOUT YOU?
YOU'RE ALL BEAT UP.

QUIT EVADING.
I'M ASKING ABOUT THAT **POWER** YOU DISPLAYED.

...

THE ENERGY EXPENDITURE WASN'T NORMAL.
ARE YOU ABSOLUTELY SURE THERE ISN'T SOME SERIOUS RISK TO USING THAT POWER?

...
WELL ...
...YOU KNOW ...

C'MON.
JUST SPILL IT!

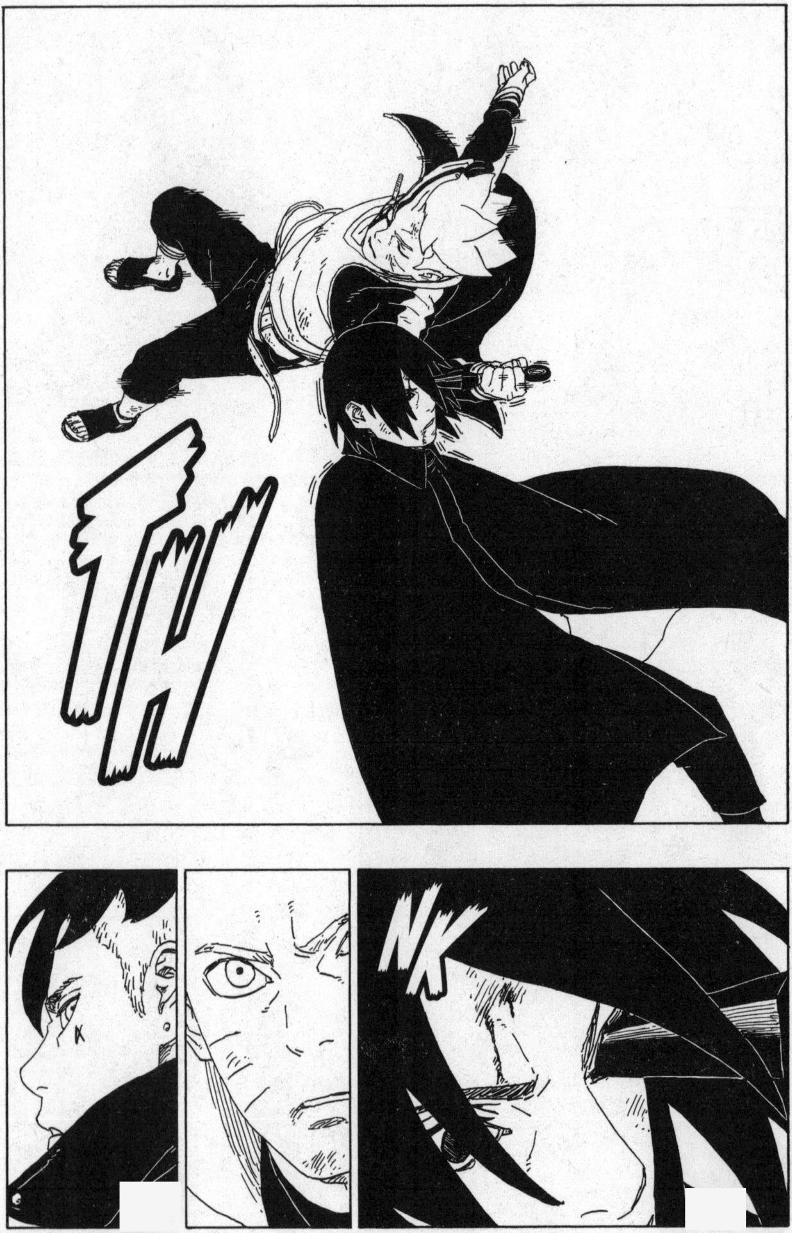

TH

NK

TMP
THDD
AARGH!!!
GUH...

OWOOOOOO

Number 54:
Bro

BORUTO
-NARUTO NEXT GENERATIONS-

VWOOOOOO

HUFF
HUFF

THERE. I'VE BLOCKED YOUR PESKY SPACE-TIME NIN-JUTSU.
THERE'S NO ESCAPE FOR YOU NOW.

MOMO-SHIKI!
HE'S COMPLETELY TAKEN OVER BORUTO'S CONSCIOUS-NESS!

THIS IS THE SECOND TIME I'VE EMERGED.
IT SURE IS NICE...
...BEING FREE.

...

LET'S GO CRUSH JIGEN!
AND THE REST OF KARA WITH HIM!

NO WAY... YOU'VE GOTTA BE KIDDING ME!
C'MON, BORUTO!!

YOU'VE BEEN FREED TOO, KAWAKI.
ISSHIKI'S SOUL HAS BEEN THOROUGHLY EXTINGUISHED.
WHERE'S YOUR SMILE?

I KNOW YOU'RE IN THERE!!
DON'T LET HIM CONTROL YOU!!
WAKE UP ALREADY!!

WELL...
...I SUPPOSE IN YOUR CASE...
...YOUR FREEDOM IS FLEETING.

RELAX.
THERE'S NOTHING YOU CAN DO.

I SAID...

SHUT UP, WHITE-EYE!!!!
STAY OUT OF THIS!!!!

GWOOSH
...SHUT UP!!!!
SLAM
SHF
WHIP

GRP
GAKK
ZWG
TAK
GWOOO

BLAM
ZWOOM

AGGH!

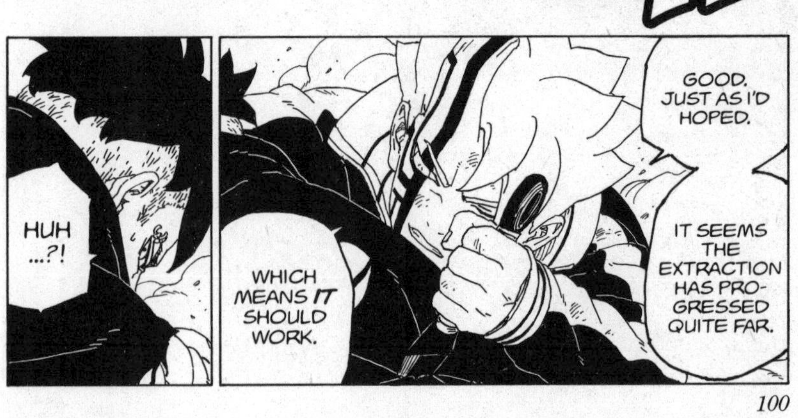

GOOD. JUST AS I'D HOPED.
IT SEEMS THE EXTRACTION HAS PRO-GRESSED QUITE FAR.
WHICH MEANS *IT* SHOULD WORK.
HUH ...?!

THOK

ARE YOU OKAY...
...KAWAKI?
NGH...
YEAH. THANKS.

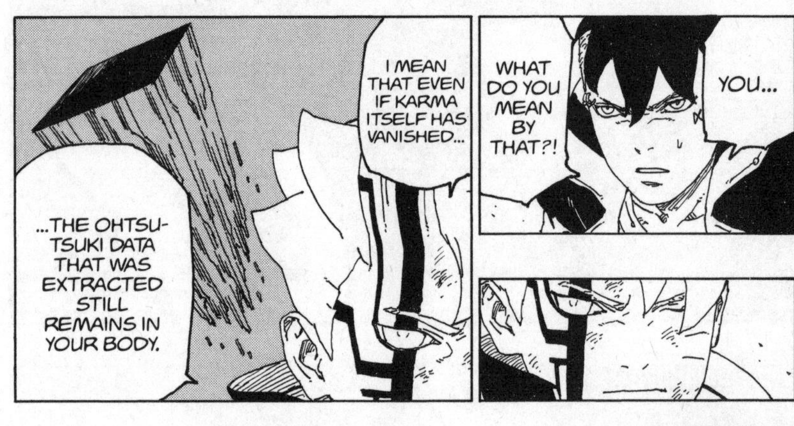
YOU...
WHAT DO YOU MEAN BY THAT?!
I MEAN THAT EVEN IF KARMA ITSELF HAS VANISHED...
...THE OHTSUTSUKI DATA THAT WAS EXTRACTED STILL REMAINS IN YOUR BODY.

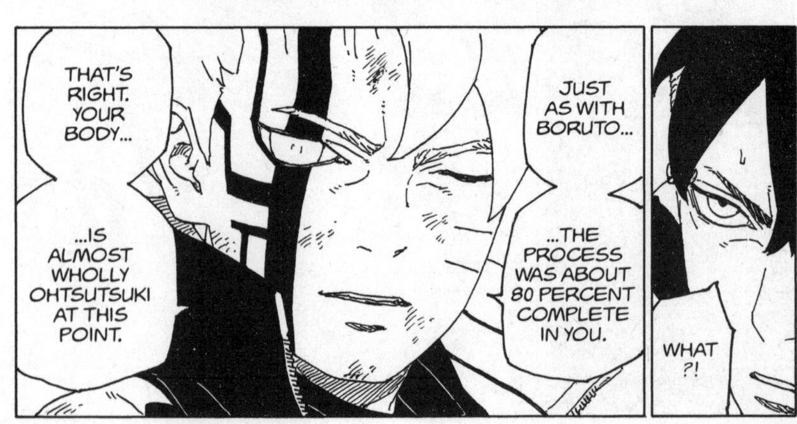
WHAT?!
JUST AS WITH BORUTO...
...THE PROCESS WAS ABOUT 80 PERCENT COMPLETE IN YOU.
THAT'S RIGHT. YOUR BODY...
...IS ALMOST WHOLLY OHTSUTSUKI AT THIS POINT.

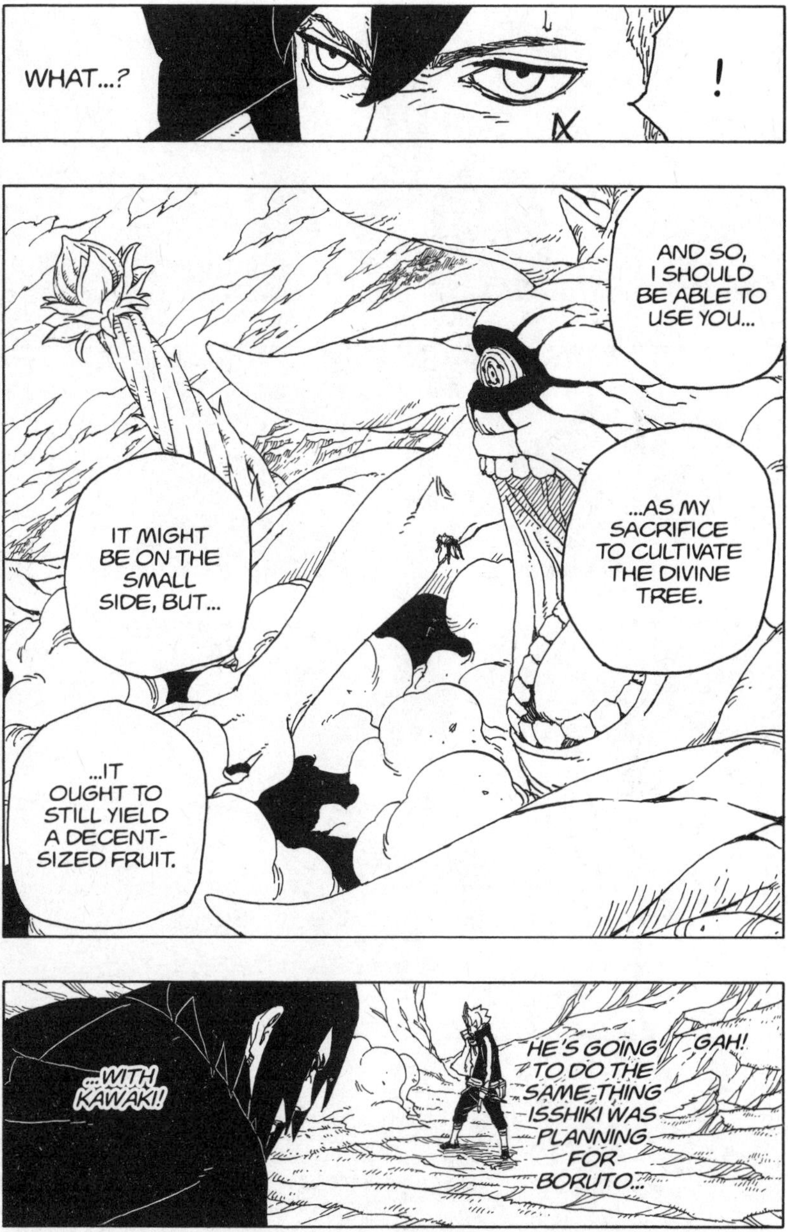

AND SO, I SHOULD BE ABLE TO USE YOU...

...AS MY SACRIFICE TO CULTIVATE THE DIVINE TREE.

IT MIGHT BE ON THE SMALL SIDE, BUT...

...IT OUGHT TO STILL YIELD A DECENT-SIZED FRUIT.

IT'S PISSING ME OFF!!!!

BOOM

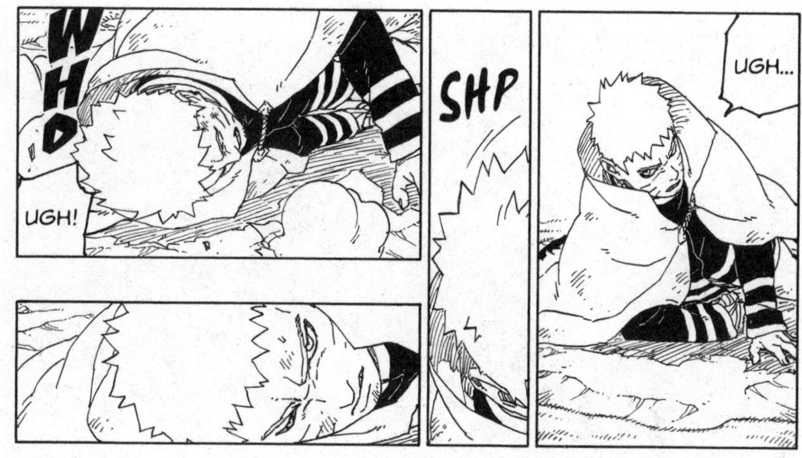
UGH...
SHP
WHD
UGH!

MY BODY...
...FEELS LIKE IT'S MADE OF LEAD.
THIS ISN'T GOOD...

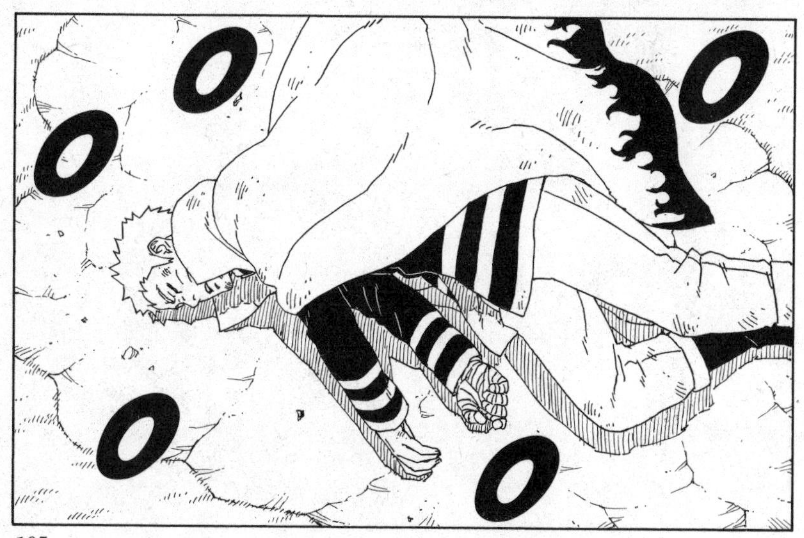
O
O
O
O
O

KLANG

... BORUTO!!
ZWISH
GKIIN
FWUP

CHING
BWAAAP
FWP FWP

ZSHH

GAH!!

...

HUH?

DO YOU REALLY INTEND...
...TO KILL YOUR FAVORITE STUDENT, UCHIHA SASUKE?

HE SHOULD'VE EASILY BEEN ABLE TO ABSORB THAT ATTACK USING KARMA.
SO WHY DIDN'T HE?

...

DON'T WORRY.
I SWEAR TO STOP YOU WITH ALL MY STRENGTH.
EVEN IF I HAVE TO KILL YOU.

YES, IF I MUST.
SHKEEN
BECAUSE I'M HIS TEACHER.
THE AMATERASU!
FWD

VWOOSH

BOOOF
TAK

HE USED THE DOPPELGANGER AS A SHIELD!

DNK
GAH!

ZSH

IF I'M NOT CAREFUL, I'LL RUN OUT OF CHAKRA FIRST.

FIRE STYLE!
VOOSH
FIREBALL TECHNIQUE!!!

KAVOOSH
TAK

!
UGH ...
HE DIDN'T ABSORB IT AGAIN.
I WONDER...

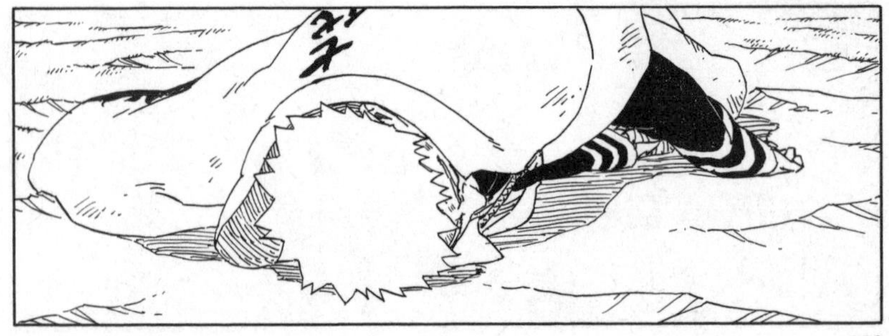

KAWA-KI!
TMP
LISTEN ...
HEY!
SOMETHING'S WRONG WITH LORD SEVENTH!
?!

HE REALLY SEEMS TO WANT TO TAKE YOU CAPTIVE FOR THE DIVINE TREE, BUT...
...AT THE SAME TIME...
...HE CAN ESCAPE FROM HERE USING SPACE-TIME NINJUTSU, AT WILL.
DON'T FORGET THAT.

DAMMIT!
I KNOW THAT!

I WANT TO GET BORUTO BACK BEFORE THAT HAPPENS.
SO WE HAVE A WAY TO RETURN TO THE VILLAGE TOO.

THAT'S EASIER SAID THAN DONE.
DO YOU HAVE A PLAN?
LISTEN.
BORUTO LOST CONSCIOUS-NESS BECAUSE HE EXPENDED TOO MUCH CHAKRA.
THERE'S A HIGH CHANCE THAT THAT'S THE DIRECT TRIGGER TO MOMOSHIKI MANIFESTING.

CON-VERSELY...
...IF WE CAN RESTORE HIS CHAKRA...
...BORUTO MAY BE ABLE TO REGAIN CONSCIOUS-NESS.

...
THAT'S A PRETTY BIG LEAP IN LOGIC.
YOU HAVE ANY PROOF?
KARMA.
HE HASN'T MADE ANY ATTEMPT TO ABSORB JUTSU USING KARMA.
PROBABLY BECAUSE HE CAN'T RISK REFILLING BORUTO'S CHAKRA.
THAT HAS TO BE IT.

VWOOOO

HE'S NOTICED.
I CAN'T LET MY GUARD DOWN WITH HIM.
HE MIGHT BE WOUNDED, BUT I STILL WON'T WALK AWAY UNHARMED IF I FACE HIM HEAD-ON.
IT'S TIME TO BRING THAT OUT...

I WANT TO TRY TO FORCE HIM TO ABSORB CHAKRA.
WITHOUT US GOING DOWN FIRST.

...

BUT THE USUAL STUFF AIN'T GONNA CUT IT.
WE MIGHT AS WELL--

ZSHHH
GAK!

KOFF!
?!

SHUP
HEH HEH. TOO WEAK TO BE A MORTAL BLOW, BUT...
...STILL MIGHTY PAINFUL IF IT HITS YOUR VITALS.

UGH! SO THAT WAS...
...BORUTO'S VANISHING RASEN-GAN!!

SHUP

I'LL GO FIND SOMETHING, OKAY?

A REPLACEMENT.

THAT GOOD ENOUGH?

THWUD

RESIST-ING IS FUTILE.
PREPARE TO GET EATEN.

ZWSHHH

IT'S NOT JUST ABOUT KARMA...
FSH

...YOU'RE TOO IMPORTANT TO ME TO LEAVE YOU BE...
...FOR ME ANYMORE, AT THIS POINT...

RIGHT?
BRO!!

DAMMIT!

YOU'RE A PAIN IN THE BUTT...

WOOSH

KAWOOOSH

!!!

WHAT THE--?!

DAMMIT!

FWAP

I'M NOT LOSING MY ONLY SACRIFICE!!

SKREEEEE

WHD

KAWAKI !!
GAH! I HAD NO CHOICE BUT TO ABSORB IT...
IT WASN'T A LOT OF CHAKRA, BUT I'VE GOT TO HURRY...
...BEFORE BORUTO WAKES UP!

SSH

VWOOOOO

BAM

GAH!!

GO BACK TO SLEEP!!

LET'S GO, KAWAKI!

FSH

IT'S TIME.

ZWOOO

WOOO

?!

WHAT THE--?!

...MOMO-SHIKI.

THAT'S ENOUGH...

G- G-
I SAID ENOUGH.
GO BACK TO YOUR HIDING PLACE.
GRP
!
YOU!!
WHAT DO YOU THINK YOU'RE--

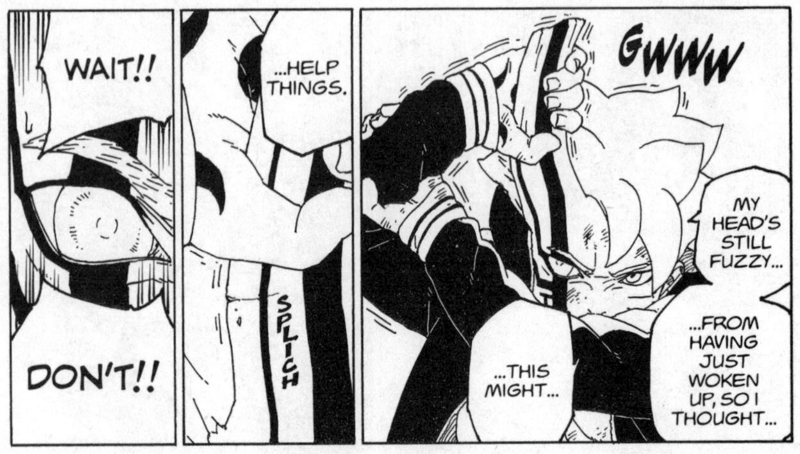
GWWW
MY HEAD'S STILL FUZZY...
...FROM HAVING JUST WOKEN UP, SO I THOUGHT...
...THIS MIGHT...
...HELP THINGS.
SPLICH
WAIT!!
DON'T!!

OW...
THUMP

SWOO

AGH...

THD

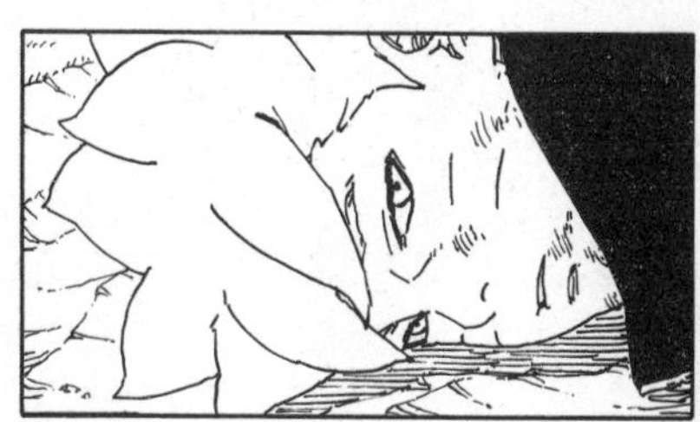

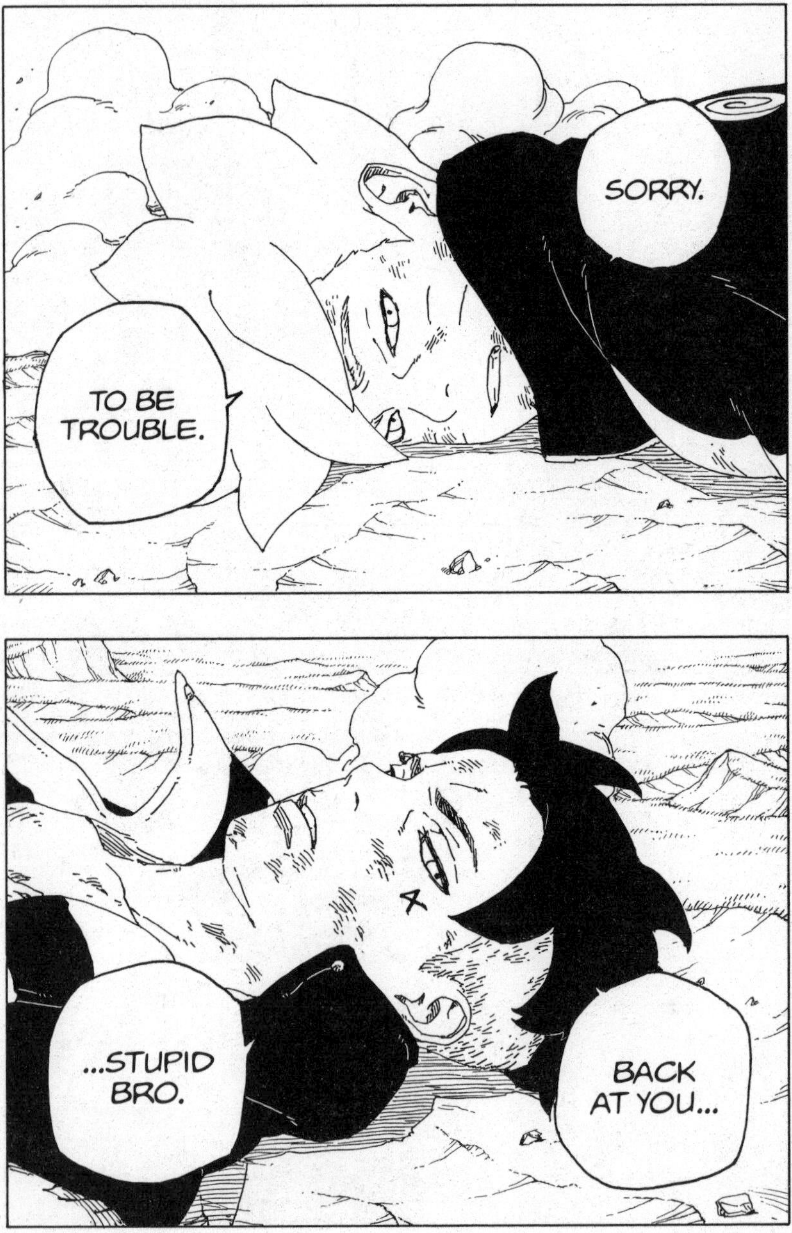

SORRY.

TO BE TROUBLE.

BACK AT YOU...

...STUPID BRO.

PHEW
...
GOOD GRIEF.

!
WHAT THE?!
NO WAY...

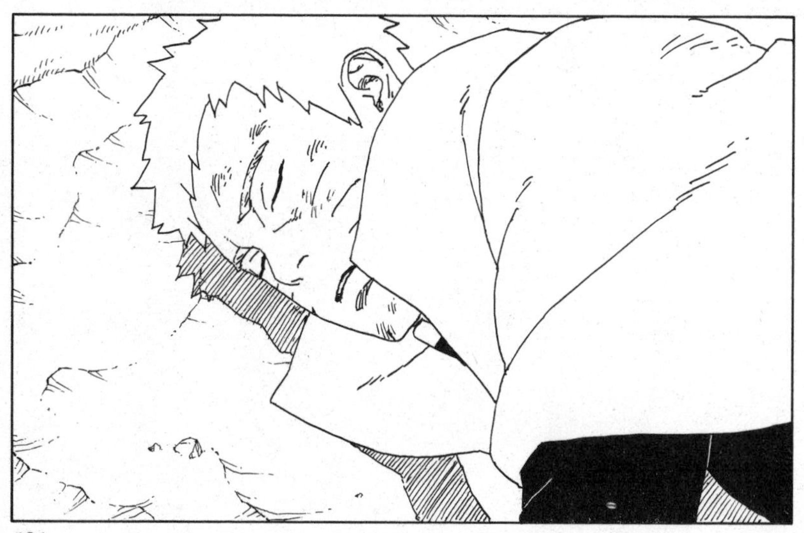

SMSH

Number 55: Legacy

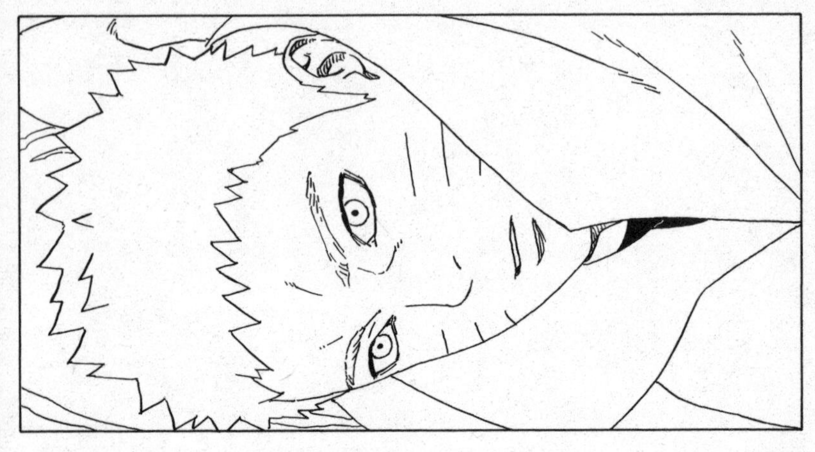

…
七代

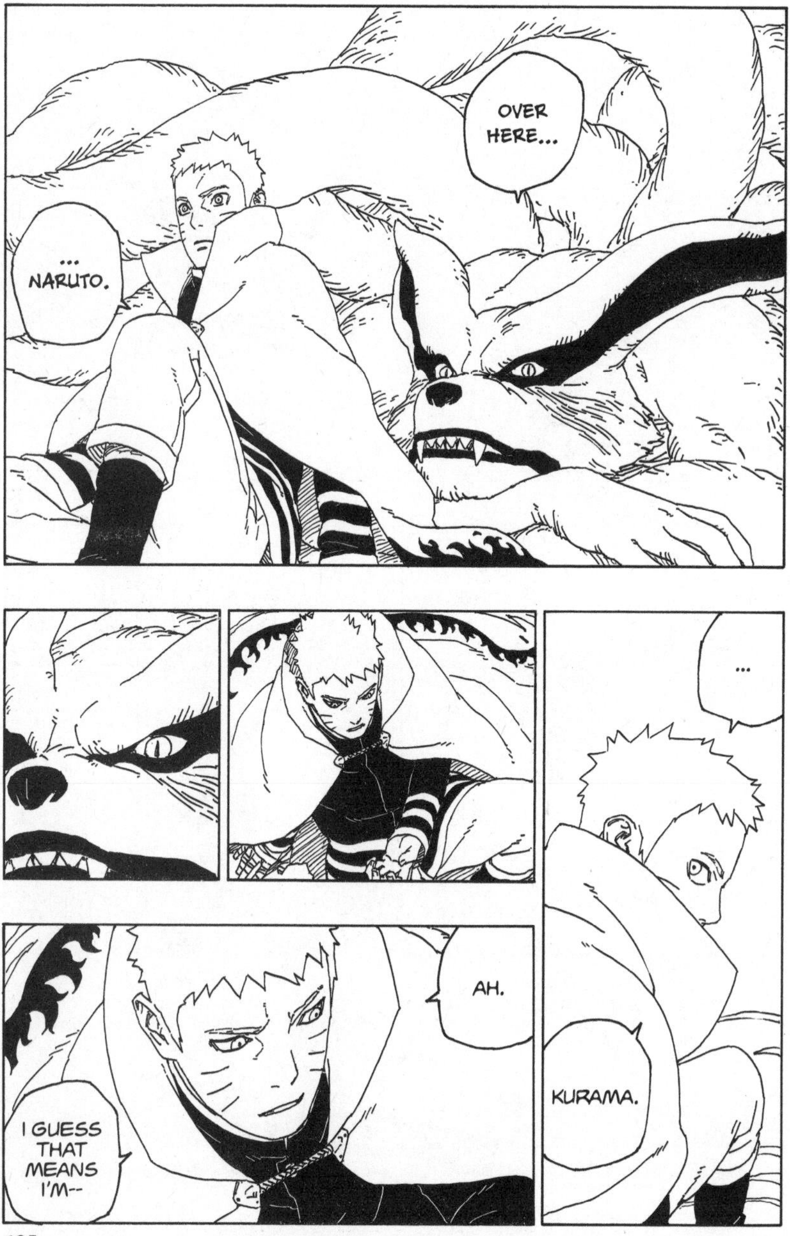

OVER HERE...

... NARUTO.

...

KURAMA.

AH.

I GUESS THAT MEANS I'M--

I CAME TO SAY FAREWELL.
SO FAR AS THAT GOES.
THIS MAY BE OUR LAST CONVERSATION.
SO START TALKING.
...
WELL...
YOU KILLED MY PA AND MA...
NO...
THAT'S NOT IT.
WE'VE BEEN THROUGH A LOT, BUT...
...ALL IN ALL, I'M REALLY GLAD YOU WERE AROUND.
THANKS.
...
ARE YOU SERIOUS?
THAT'S IT?

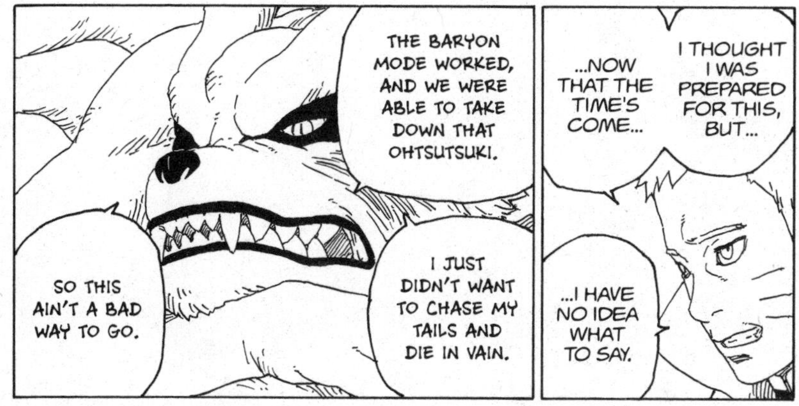
I THOUGHT I WAS PREPARED FOR THIS, BUT...
...NOW THAT THE TIME'S COME...
...I HAVE NO IDEA WHAT TO SAY.
THE BARYON MODE WORKED, AND WE WERE ABLE TO TAKE DOWN THAT OHTSUTSUKI.
I JUST DIDN'T WANT TO CHASE MY TAILS AND DIE IN VAIN.
SO THIS AIN'T A BAD WAY TO GO.

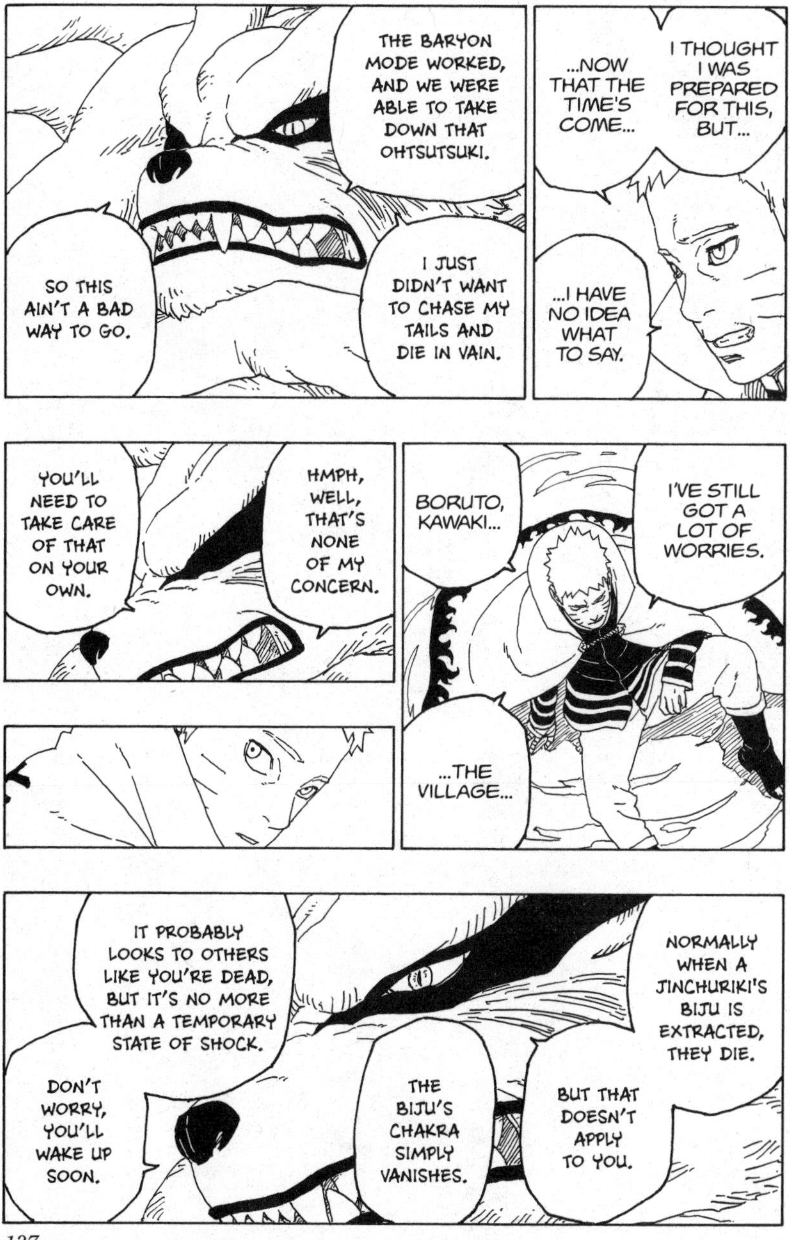

I'VE STILL GOT A LOT OF WORRIES.
BORUTO, KAWAKI...
...THE VILLAGE...
HMPH, WELL, THAT'S NONE OF MY CONCERN.
YOU'LL NEED TO TAKE CARE OF THAT ON YOUR OWN.

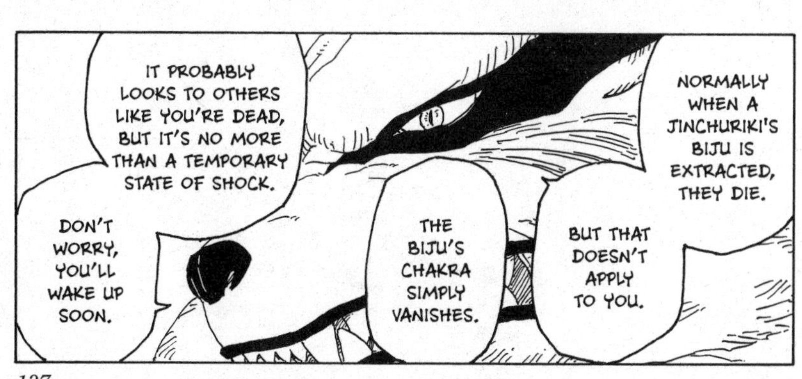
NORMALLY WHEN A JINCHURIKI'S BIJU IS EXTRACTED, THEY DIE.
BUT THAT DOESN'T APPLY TO YOU.
THE BIJU'S CHAKRA SIMPLY VANISHES.
IT PROBABLY LOOKS TO OTHERS LIKE YOU'RE DEAD, BUT IT'S NO MORE THAN A TEMPORARY STATE OF SHOCK.
DON'T WORRY, YOU'LL WAKE UP SOON.

...!
HOLD ON...
WAIT A SEC.
WHAT ARE YOU SAYING?!

THE BARYON MODE'S PRICE IS **MY** LIFE.
NOT YOURS, NARUTO.

JUST SO YOU KNOW, I NEVER ONCE LIED TO YOU.
AT NO TIME DID I EVER SAY THAT YOU WOULD DIE.
YOU--!
YOU DELIBER-ATELY MISLED ME!

IF I'D TOLD YOU AT THE GET-GO THAT THIS POWER...
...CAME IN EXCHANGE FOR MY LIFE, YOU WOULD'VE HESITATED.
OR WORSE, OPPOSED IT OUTRIGHT.
EVEN IF YOU KNEW IT WAS OUR ONLY HOPE.
CUZ YOU'RE ANNOYING LIKE THAT.
AM I WRONG?
...
TCH.
DON'T LOOK AT ME LIKE THAT.
PSHHH
THAT'S WHAT'S ANNOYING ABOUT YOU.
WELL, I GUESS THIS IS IT.
I'VE GOT TO GO, BUT...
...BE REAL CAREFUL. YOU AIN'T GONNA HAVE SUPERHUMAN STRENGTH ANYMORE.
SO IF YOU OVERDO IT, YOU'LL END UP JOINING ME IN NO TIME.
KURAMA!

BUT UNTIL THAT DAY COMES...
...YOU BE WELL...
...NARUTO.

WAIT...
DON'T GO!
KURA-MA!!

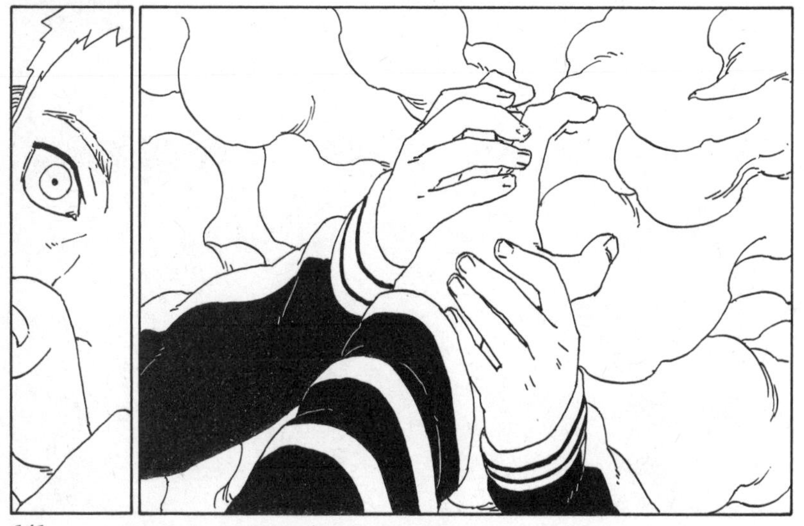

DAD!!

...!
BO-RUTO?
...
SNIFF ...
!!

WAAAH !!!
GWOM
HOW COULD YOU WORRY ME LIKE THAT?!
STUPID DAD!!!
UNH.
OWW!
HEY, WATCH IT!

WMP
...
SIGH...

VWOOO
I SEE.
SO KURAMA'S ...
I ASSUMED I'D BE THE ONE WHO WOULD DIE.
THOUGH I SUPPOSE KURAMA WOULD STILL BE DEAD THEN TOO.
I NEVER THOUGHT IT'D END UP LIKE THIS.
NOT TO BE RUDE, BUT...
...CAN WE TALK ABOUT THIS...
...*AFTER* WE GET HOME?
OH, RIGHT.
SORRY.
LET'S GET GOING.
BORUTO.
CAN YOU DO IT?
HUH?

M-ME?!

YOU MEAN, USING THIS?

YES.

I CAN'T USE MY RINNEGAN ANYMORE.

UH...

...

MASTER...

DON'T WORRY ABOUT IT. I'M JUST STATING A FACT.

THIS IS ***NOT*** YOUR FAULT.

WE WERE ALL PREPARED TO DIE.

WE NEED TO COUNT OURSELVES LUCKY TO HAVE WON AND SURVIVED.

THE MAN HIMSELF IS TELLING YOU IT'S OKAY, SO DROP IT.

JUST HURRY UP AND DO IT, BORUTO.

SINCE THERE AIN'T NO OTHER WAY.

SHADDUP! I KNOW THAT!

I NEED A MOMENT, ALL RIGHT?!

VWOOOOOO

ZZZ...
ZZZ...
FLIK

GWP

YAAAWN...

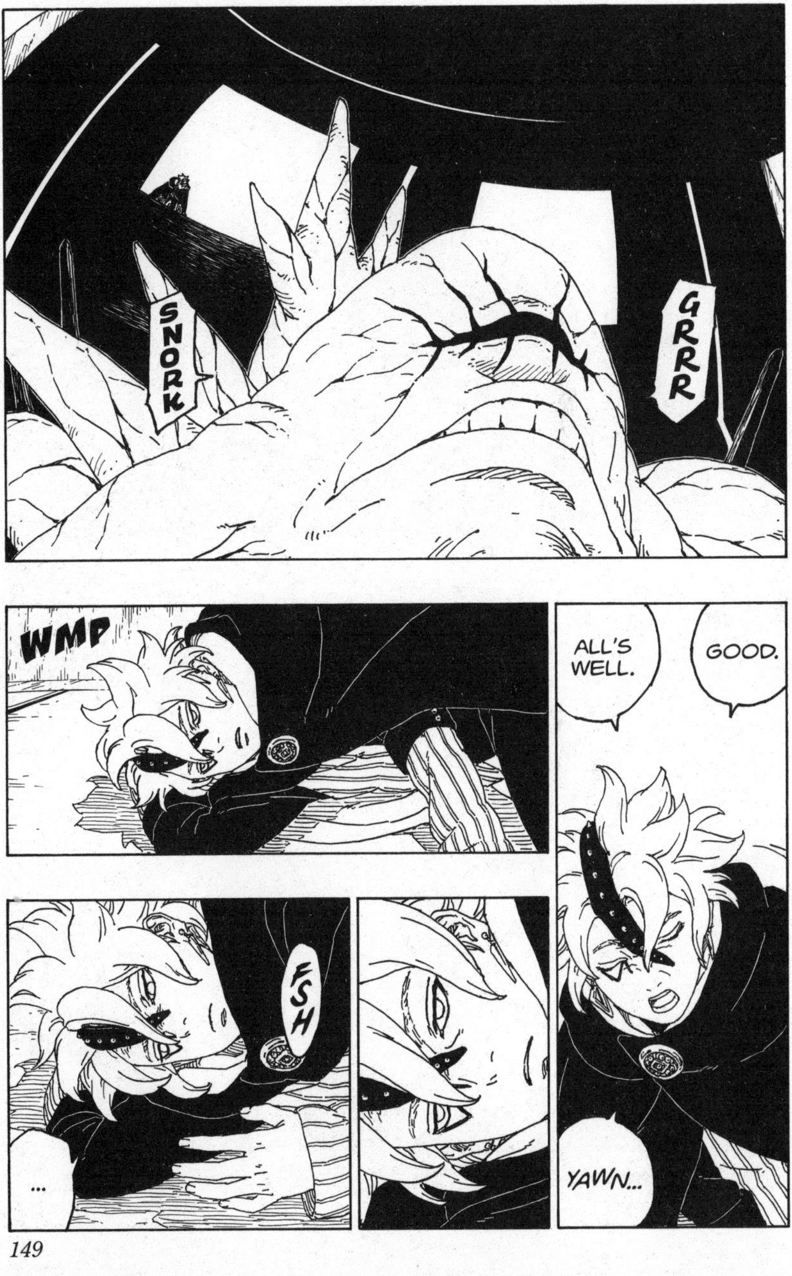

GRRR
SNORK
GOOD.
ALL'S WELL.
YAWN...
WMP
FSH
...

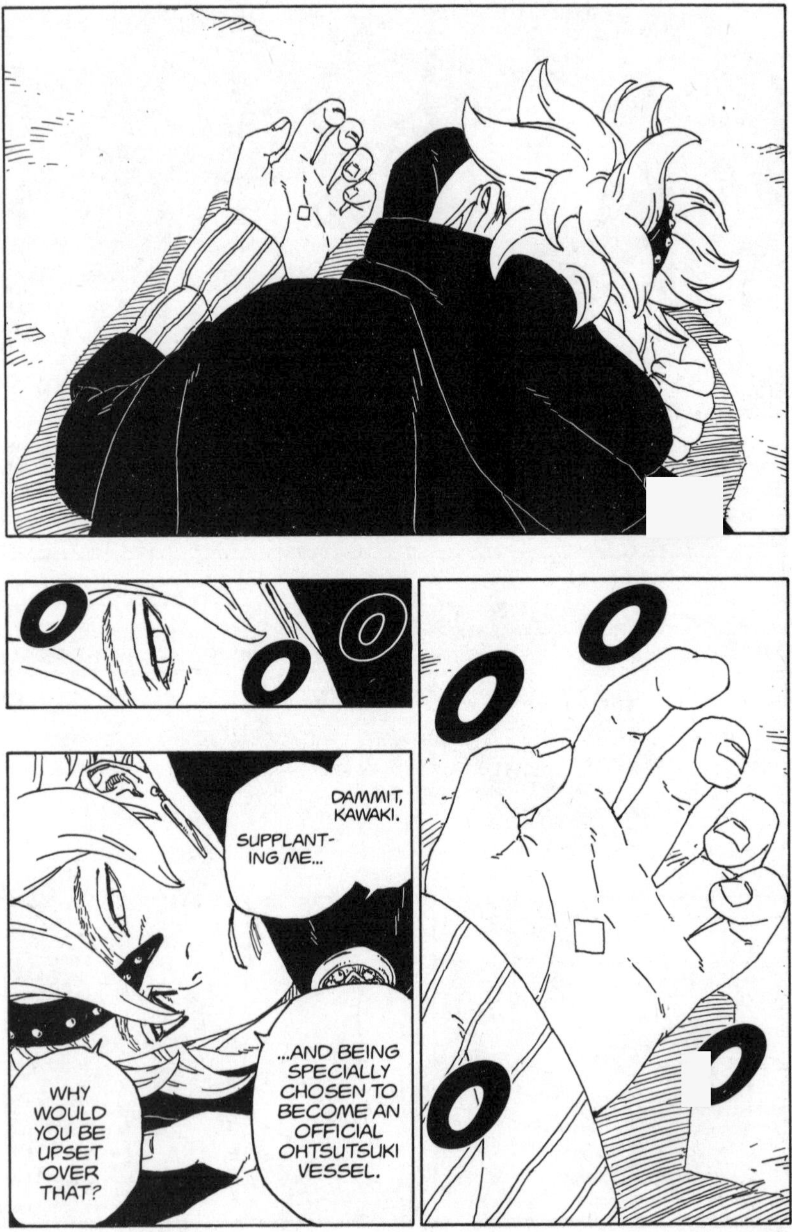

DAMMIT, KAWAKI.

SUPPLANTING ME...

...AND BEING SPECIALLY CHOSEN TO BECOME AN OFFICIAL OHTSUTSUKI VESSEL.

WHY WOULD YOU BE UPSET OVER THAT?

I WOULDN'T WASTE THE OPPORTUNITY.
IF I'D ACTUALLY HAD A REAL KARMA...
...INSTEAD OF THIS DUD.
KEEN
BOF
B-BBOF
?!
B-B-BBOF
VWOOOO

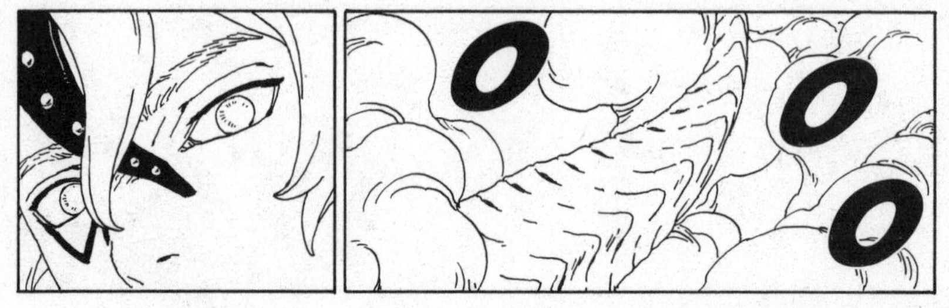

CODE.

MY MOST LOYAL, BELOVED SERVANT.

...!

YOU'RE ...

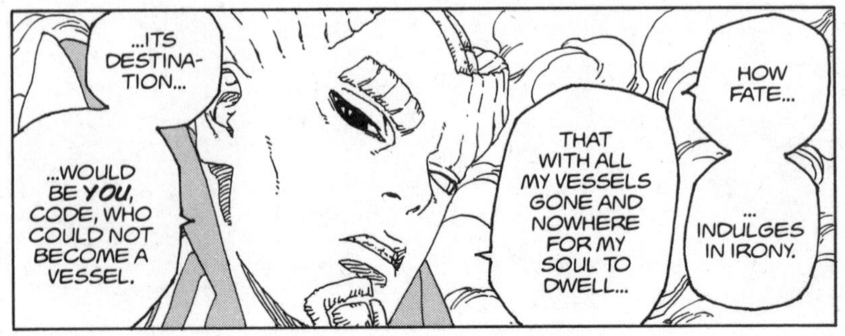
HOW FATE...
...INDULGES IN IRONY.
THAT WITH ALL MY VESSELS GONE AND NOWHERE FOR MY SOUL TO DWELL...
...ITS DESTINATION...
...WOULD BE **YOU**, CODE, WHO COULD NOT BECOME A VESSEL.

YOUR SOUL?
THE RESURRECTION FAILED?!
WHAT HAPPENED TO KAWAKI?
I WAS DECEIVED AND BETRAYED BY AMADO, AND WAS FORCED TO RESURRECT IN JIGEN.
AND THUS, ENDED UP LIKE SO.
IT CAUSED KAWAKI'S KARMA TO DISSIPATE, BUT...
...IT APPEARS YOUR KARMA HAS REMAINED, YOU WHO WERE NOT SUITABLE TO BE A VESSEL.

BUT THIS KARMA IS A DUD.
UNLIKE KAWAKI, I COULDN'T BECOME A VESSEL.
I AM BEYOND HUMBLED THAT YOU HAVE APPEARED BEFORE ME, BUT...
...UNFORTUNATELY, I CANNOT SERVE AS A RECEPTACLE FOR YOUR SOUL.

MY SOUL WILL DISSIPATE SHORTLY.

BUT I CANNOT ALLOW THE OHTSUTSUKI WILL TO BE SNUFFED OUT AS WELL.

NOT WHEN WE HAVE DEVOURED COUNTLESS PLANETS...

...AND CONTINUOUSLY EVOLVED OVER THOUSANDS OF YEARS...

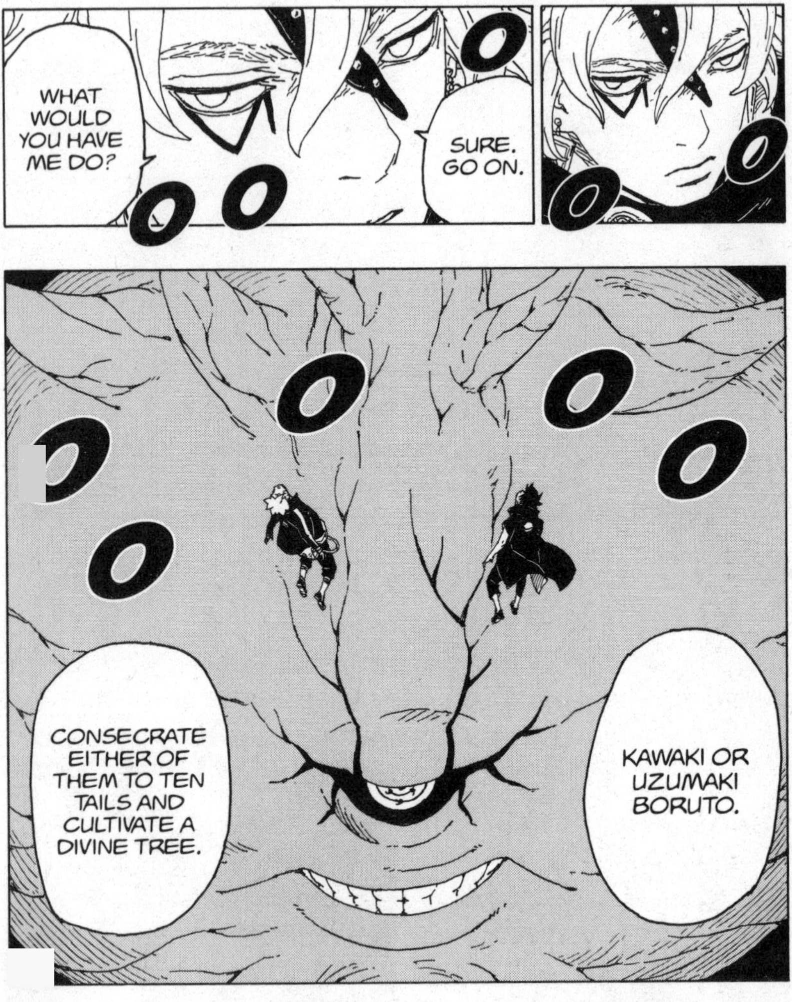

KAWAKI OR UZUMAKI BORUTO.

CONSECRATE EITHER OF THEM TO TEN TAILS AND CULTIVATE A DIVINE TREE.

EAT IT AND UPGRADE YOURSELF, CODE.

DO THAT...

...AND YOU YOUR-SELF WILL BECOME A NEW OHTSU-TSUKI.

THEN GO FORTH AND DEVOUR...

...PLANET AFTER PLANET ACROSS SPACE.

KEEP EVOLVING...

...UNTIL YOU BECOME A PEERLESS, UNIQUE EXISTENCE.

A GOD.

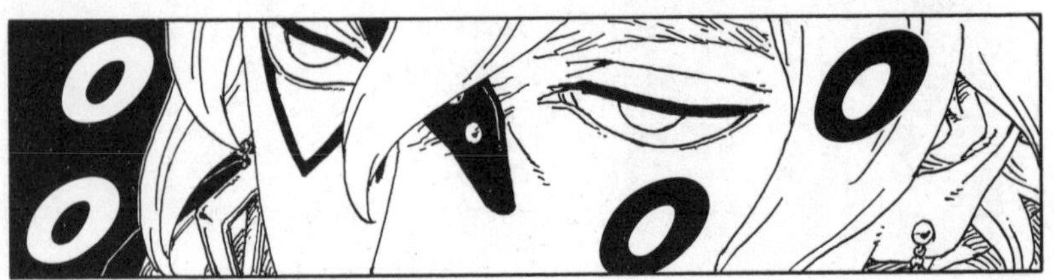

SO FIRST I WANT TO DISPOSE OF...

...THOSE WHO STOLE THE PILLAR OF MY HEART FROM ME.

ZWWW

BEFORE I HAVE THE DIVINE TREE ABSORB ALL LIFE.

TELL ME...

...THE NAMES OF THE BASTARDS WHO DESTROYED YOU.

VWOOO
RRR...
GAH!!

LOOSEN UP. YOU'RE STIFF AS A BOARD.
IT SHOULD BE EASY IF YOU RELAX.
ARE YOU SCARED...
...THAT **HE** WILL EMERGE AGAIN?

...
...
I NEVER WANT TO EXPERIENCE THAT AGAIN.
BUT...
...I HONESTLY CAN'T...
...GUARANTEE THAT IT WON'T HAPPEN.

IT'S THE SAME WITH YOU.

YOU AIN'T LIKELY TO SOLVE IT ALL ON YOUR OWN.

SO STOP THINKING ABOUT IT.

THAT'S EASY FOR YOU TO SAY!

I'LL SOMEHOW GET RID OF YOUR KARMA...

I SWEAR IT.

!
KAWA-KI...
WE PROMISED TO HELP EACH OTHER, REMEMBER?
IT'S NOT OVER JUST CUZ MINE'S GONE.
I'M NOT STOPPING UNTIL WE TAKE CARE OF YOURS TOO.
SHUP

I SUFFERED FROM THE KARMA FOR YEARS.
IT AIN'T MEANT AS A BOAST, BUT I'M A LOT MORE SEASONED THAN YOU.
SO I ABSOLUTELY *HATE* KARMA...
...FROM THE BOTTOM OF MY HEART.
SHUP
AND I WON'T REST...
...UNTIL I STAMP THEM ALL OUT, NO MATTER WHO HAS IT.

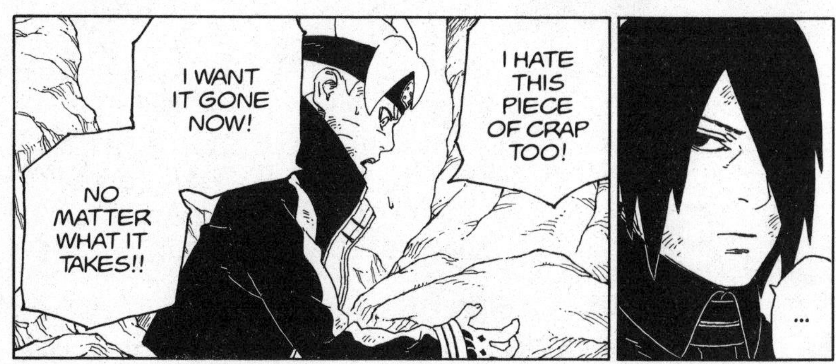
...
I HATE THIS PIECE OF CRAP TOO!
I WANT IT GONE NOW!
NO MATTER WHAT IT TAKES!!

QUIT FREAKIN' OUT AND JUST HURRY UP AND DO IT, YOU IDIOT!!!

HUH?!!

WHAT GIVES YOU THE RIGHT TO BOSS ME AROUND LIKE THAT?!!

WHA ?!

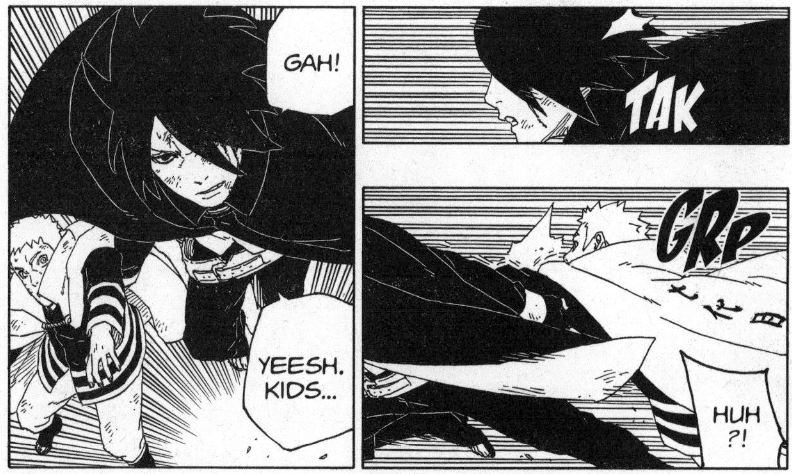

FWOOO

NO... NOT YET.
NOT WHILE THE SITUATION STILL ISN'T CLEAR.
...
WHO KNOWS? I CAN'T SAY.
JUST TELL THEM TO KEEP DOING THEIR JOBS.

DEAR ME.
HOW ARE THINGS GOING TO TURN OUT?
ANY THOUGHTS ...
...DR. AMADO?

...
MUTTER

MUTTER MUTTER

...
DR. AMADO ...?

!
OH, SORRY.
YOU WERE SAYING?

...
NO, NO.
NOTHING IMPORTANT.

...
OH?

...

WHAT?!
YOU'RE SURE?
YEAH...
AND OHTSUTSUKI?!
...
I SEE. ALL RIGHT.
RUSH THE MEDIC CORPS THERE.
WE'LL FOLLOW RIGHT BEHIND.

NARUTO AND THE OTHERS ARE BACK!
AHH!
AND NO SIGN OF OHTSUTSUKI.
IT LOOKS LIKE THINGS WENT WELL.
HEY!
WHAT ABOUT KAWAKI?
IS HE OKAY?!
I'M TOLD THEY'RE ALL INJURED BUT SAFE.
IN ANY CASE, WE'RE HEADED THERE NOW.
WE'LL KNOW MORE THEN.

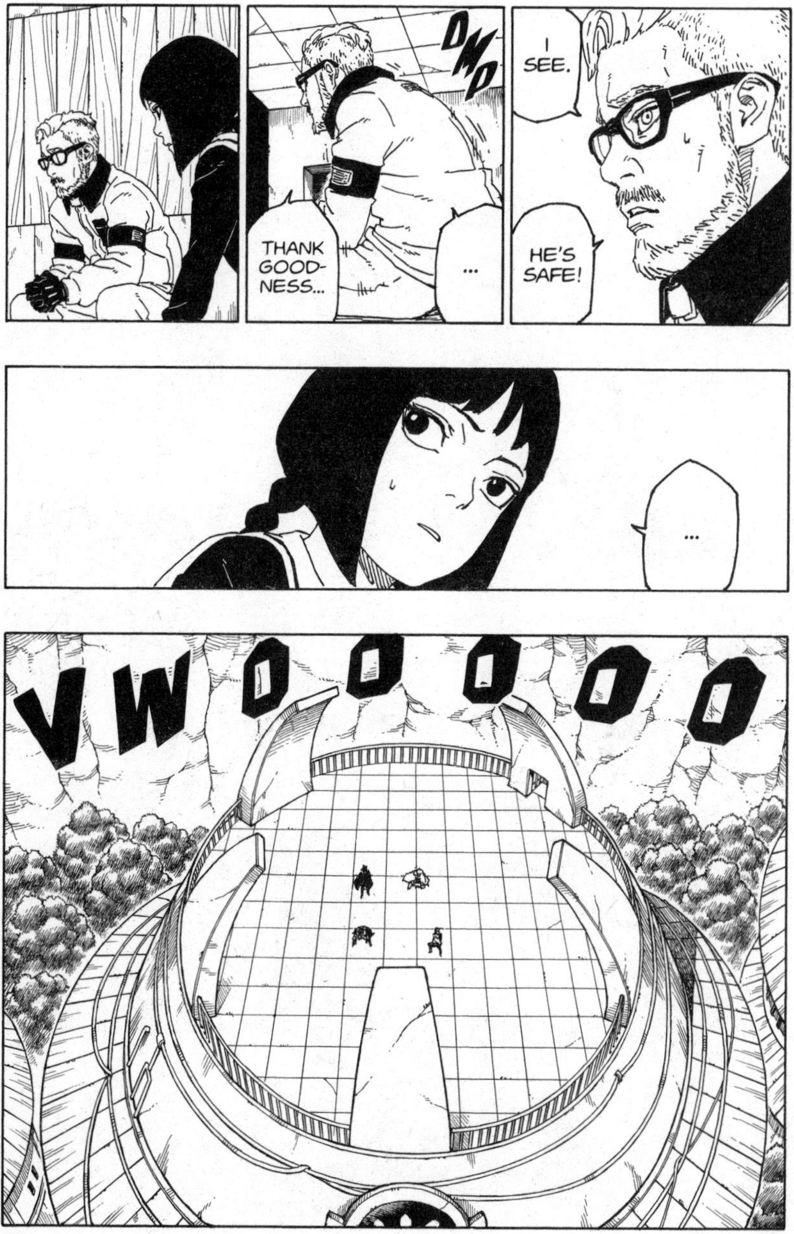

I SEE.
HE'S SAFE!

DMP
...
THANK GOODNESS...

...

VWOOOO

PHEW!!
I'M BEAT...
AH...
FINALLY HOME.
TO OUR VILLAGE.
YEAH.
BARELY, BUT SOMEHOW...
...

...I DO FEEL LIKE ANYTHING'S POSSIBLE...

...AS LONG AS I'M WITH YOU.

YOU GOTTA BE JOKING.

HURRY UP AND STAND ON YOUR OWN.

GAH.

VW

...MOMO-SHIKI'S VESSEL...

...UZUMAKI BORUTO.

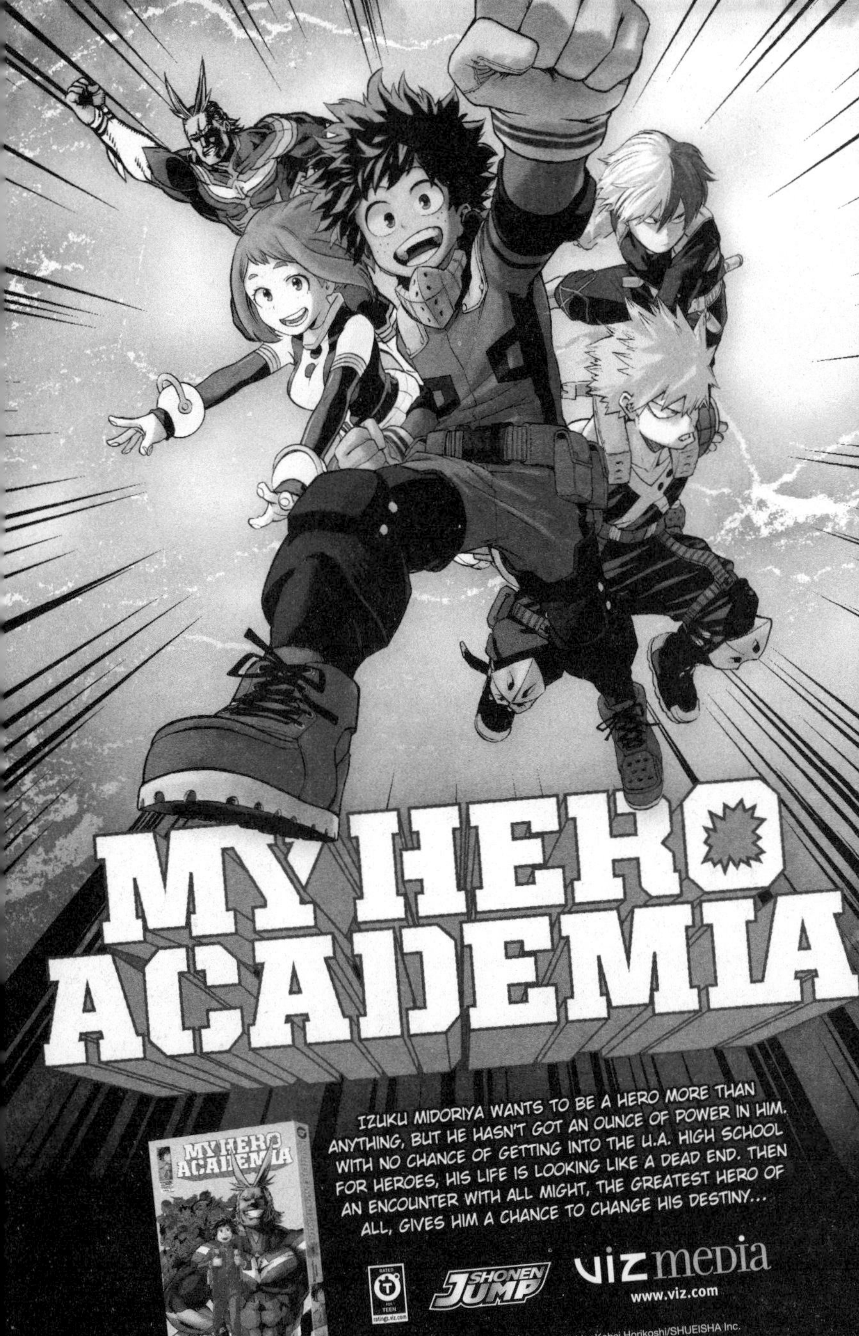
MY HERO ACADEMIA
IZUKU MIDORIYA WANTS TO BE A HERO MORE THAN ANYTHING, BUT HE HASN'T GOT AN OUNCE OF POWER IN HIM. WITH NO CHANCE OF GETTING INTO THE U.A. HIGH SCHOOL FOR HEROES, HIS LIFE IS LOOKING LIKE A DEAD END. THEN AN ENCOUNTER WITH ALL MIGHT, THE GREATEST HERO OF ALL, GIVES HIM A CHANCE TO CHANGE HIS DESTINY...
MY HERO ACADEMIA
KOHEI HORIKOSHI
RATED T TEEN
ratings.viz.com
SHONEN JUMP
VIZ media
www.viz.com
BOKU NO HERO ACADEMIA © 2014 by Kohei Horikoshi/SHUEISHA Inc.

YOU'RE READING IN THE WRONG DIRECTION!!

WHOOPS! Guess what? You're starting at the wrong end of the comic!

...It's true! In keeping with the original Japanese format, **Boruto** is meant to be read from right to left, starting in the upper-right corner.

Unlike English, which is read from left to right, Japanese is read from right to left, meaning that action, sound effects, and word-balloon order are completely reversed... something which can make readers unfamiliar with Japanese feel pretty backwards themselves. For this reason, manga or Japanese comics published in the U.S. in English have sometimes been published "flopped"—that is, printed in exact reverse order, as though seen from the other side of a mirror.

By flopping pages, U.S. publishers can avoid confusing readers, but the compromise is not without its downside. For one thing, a character in a flopped manga series who once wore in the original Japanese version a T-shirt emblazoned with "M A Y" (as in "the merry month of") now wears one which reads "Y A M"! Additionally, many manga creators in Japan are themselves unhappy with the process, as some feel the mirror-imaging of their art alters their original intentions.

We are proud to bring you **Boruto** in the original unflopped format. Turn to the other side of the book and let the ninjutsu begin...!

—Editor

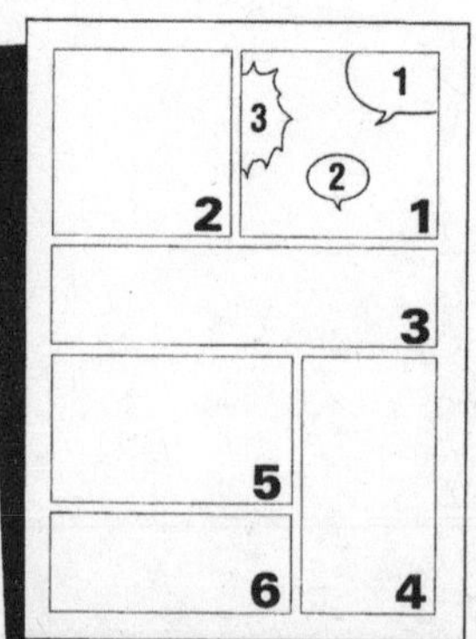